LEARNING THROUGH A PRISM

Facilitating Student Intercultural Learning Abroad

TRACY RUNDSTROM WILLIAMS

TCU Press
FORT WORTH, TEXAS

Library of Congress Cataloging-in-Publication Data

Names: Williams, Tracy Rundstrom, 1974- author.

Title: Learning through a PRISM : facilitating student intercultural learning abroad / Tracy Williams.

Description: Fort Worth, Texas : TCU Press, [2018] |

Identifiers: LCCN 2018001358 (print) | LCCN 2018004343 (ebook) | ISBN 9780875656977 | ISBN 9780875656908 | ISBN 9780875656908? (alk. paper)

Subjects: LCSH: Foreign study—Study and teaching (Higher). | Cultural competence—Study and teaching (Higher). | Multicultural education.

Classification: LCC LB2375 (ebook) | LCC LB2375 .W54 2018 (print) | DDC 370.116—dc23

LC record available at https://urldefense.proofpoint.com/v2/url?u=https-3A__lccn.loc.gov_2018001358&d=DwIFAg&c=7Q-FWLBTAxn3T_E3HWrzGYJrC4RvUoWDrz-TlitGRH_A&r=O2eiy819IcwTGuw-vrBGiVdmhQxMh2yxeggw9qlTUDE&m=CVp-J2s75pvy1euTy1LAJogaln9j_4pSTQWRY-paIKTc&s=DiSJNBapxQ7wE5TaAmqbJ-HRNyVZCgbRakpGIualdZvw&e=

TCU Press
TCU Box 298300
Fort Worth, Texas 76129
817.257.7822
www.prs.tcu.edu
To order books: 1.800.826.8911

Cover and Text Design by Preston Thomas

LEARNING THROUGH A PRISM

To my father, Jim Rundstrom, who models openness, flexibility, curiosity, and empathy every day, I am grateful for your guidance, support, and for our many wonderful travels together.

"It's not our differences that divide us.
It is our inability to recognize, accept,
and celebrate those differences."

AUDRE LORDE

CONTENTS

FOREWORD

Intercultural competence has emerged prominently within international education in the last decade as evidenced by the IAU Survey on Internationalization (Egron-Polak and Hudson) and the European Parliament Study (de Wit et al, 2015), both of which indicate the centrality of intercultural learning outcomes within internationalization efforts. Institutions of higher education increasingly understand the value and importance of focusing on intercultural and global learning, both on campus and in education abroad programs. One example of this is the work of the Association of American Colleges and Universities on the Intercultural VALUE rubric (among other rubrics including a global learning rubric), which was developed by faculty from across the US and described more fully here in Learning Through a PRISM. The theoretical basis of this rubric is Bennett's Developmental Model of Intercultural Sensitivity (1993) and my Intercultural Competence models (Deardorff, 2006), which are the first grounded research-based ICC frameworks. Outlining only six components of the very complex concept of intercultural competence, this rubric is meant to serve as an example that can be further adapted, depending on institutional and programmatic contexts, as this book models. Recognizing that intercultural competence development is a lifelong process (Deardorff, 2009), scholars including Tracy Williams remind educators of the importance of helping students hone intercultural learning that will carry them through a myriad of diverse experiences throughout their lives.

With all the research and scholarly efforts around intercultural competence development and assessment, one question persists: How exactly can intercultural competence be developed? Tracy Williams joins various scholars who have responded to this question. For example, J. Bennett (2009) outlines a four-step process that involves "fostering attitudes that motivate us, discovering knowledge that informs us of our own and others' cultural positions, assessing the challenge and support factors that affect our adaption, and developing skills that enable us to interact effectively and appropriately" (p. 125). Other scholars describe three key themes in intercultural competence development: 1) the acquisition of a combination of specific knowledge, skills, and attitudes; 2) a recognition of the developmental nature of intercultural competence (meaning a progression from more ethnocentric worldviews toward a more global mindset); and 3) a focus on the process of learning (Gregersen-Hermans and Pusch, 2012, p. 23-24). In addition to this scholarly work, there are various practical resources that have been published which contain specific learning activities designed to develop intercultural competence such as *Building Cultural Competence: Innovative Activities and Models* (Berardo and Deardorff, 2012) or *TASKs for Democracy: 60 Activities to Learn and Assess Transversal Attitudes, Skills, and Knowledge* from the Council of Europe (Mompoint-Gaillard and Lazar, 2015).

This new publication by Tracy Williams is unique in that it provides both academic and practical information for faculty so that they can be better positioned to help guide students' intercultural development within the context of an education abroad program. As the author states in her introduction, "intercultural competence development needs to be given as much attention and intentionality as goals to increase numbers of participants, ensure students have healthy and safe experiences, and provide internationalization opportunities for more faculty." Certainly, this manual not only helps emphasize the importance of intercultural learning within an experience abroad, but also serves as a catalyst for further conversations on this epicenter of student transformation.

Darla K. Deardorff
Duke University
February 2017

Bennett, J. (2009). Cultivating intercultural competence: A process perspective. In D. K. Deardorff (Ed.), *The Sage handbook of intercultural competence*. Thousand Oaks, CA: Sage

Bennett, M. (1993). Towards ethnorelativism: A developmental model of intercultural sensitivity. In R. M. Paige (Ed.), *Education for the intercultural experience* (pp. 21–71). Yarmouth, ME: Intercultural Press.

Berardo, K. and Deardorff, D.K. (2012). *Building cultural competence: Innovative activities and models*. Sterling, VA: Stylus

De Wit, H., Hunter, F., Howard, L. and Egron-Polak, E. (2015). *Internationalisation of Higher Education* a global study commissioned by the European Parliament. Brussels: European Parliament

Deardorff, D.K. (2006). The identification and assessment of intercultural competence as a student outcome of internationalization at institutions of higher education in the United States. *Journal of Studies in International Education 10:241-266*

Deardorff, D.K. (2009). *The Sage handbook of intercultural competence.* Thousand Oaks, CA: Sage

Egron-Polak, E. and and Hudson, R. (2014*). Internationalization of higher education : growing expectations, fundamental values. IAU global survey.* Paris; International Association of Universities

Gregersen-Hermans, J. and Pusch, P. (2012). How to design and assess an intercultural learning experience. In K. Berardo and D. Deardorff (Eds), *Building cultural competence: Innovative activities and models.* Sterling, VA: Stylus

Mompoint-Gaillard, P. and Lazar, I., (2015). *TASKs for democracy: 60 activities to learn and assess transversal attitudes, skills, and knowledge.* Strasbourg: Council of Europe. Available at http://www.coe.int/t/dg4/education/pestalozzi/Source/Documentation/Pestalozzi4_EN.pdf

PREFACE

In the twenty-five years since I first studied abroad myself, I have seen a number of changes in the field of international education: the professionalization of the field, an increased focus on outcomes, an increased attention to student needs, shorter periods of time abroad, an increased focus on risk management, and perhaps most relevant for this manual, a greater variety of educators involved, including faculty and administrators who have different levels of knowledge and experience.

Amidst all the changes and growth, one theme has remained constant: studying abroad provides students tremendous learning *opportunities* to gain knowledge about the country they visit and the culture of its people, awareness of different perspectives and empathy for others, flexibility, emotional resilience, and communication skills. These qualities have come to be called "intercultural competence" and stand as markers for the many skills universities expect from students as "global-ready graduates" or global citizens.

Unfortunately, there is a disconnect between what students *could* learn from studying abroad and what they *actually* learn.

Generally speaking, research has shown students need guidance and programs need intentionality in order to convert opportunities and experiences into knowledge. Students need nudging and prompting to get out of their comfort zones and experiment, and they need structure to process and interpret their experiences. Students need assistance to draw lessons from their experiences, articulate what they have gained, and create relevance and meaning.

Educators need assistance too. Administrators, faculty, and staff need a framework to facilitate and measure students' intercultural competence. Many come with their own lens of how international layers onto their field, or what skills they hope students gain, but the interdisciplinary integration of anthropology, sociology, linguistics, communication, and psychology, which I call the field of intercultural learning, is just emerging. Outside of a few degree programs and institutes, there has not been a systematic approach to training educators in intercultural learning, leading to a lack of grounding for learning objectives and, understandably, inconsistent student achievement of those fairly undefined learning objectives. We may know what we want, but until we have a pedagogical framework dedicated to intercultural competence, we cannot give our students the tools to achieve this.

The lack of pedagogical framework is further complicated by the fact that administrators, faculty, and staff are often faced with goals for education abroad that seem to work against improving intercultural competence. While they are important elements, goals such as increasing student numbers and ensuring students have healthy and safe experiences can lead to sterile, Americanized programs that lack meaningful intercultural interactions. In addition, goals such as providing more opportunities for faculty to teach abroad can result in faculty leaders with little or no training in intercultural development and faculty frustration with this lack of training. Ultimately, focusing more on quantitative outcomes has meant that the development of students' intercultural competence has not been fully realized.

Quantitative goals do not have to be incompatible with intercultural learning goals, but the development of intercultural competence needs to be given as much attention and intentionality as goals to increase the number of participants, ensure students have healthy and safe experiences, and provide internationalization opportunities for more faculty. How do we do this? Who has time to do this? There are so many other components of the education abroad experience that faculty and staff need to focus on: for faculty, their own academic course content in the new site; for staff, the program administration and management, student health and safety preparation and response, and student advising and preparation.

A pedagogy dedicated to intercultural learning in study abroad programs is needed. Many have worked on developing such a pedagogy—a "study abroad training course." Bruce LaBrack pioneered some of the first and most successful predeparture and reentry courses in the 1990s and eventually put his training models online in the "What's Up With Culture" resource (2003), although his work has focused more on the predeparture and reentry phases of study abroad experiences. After the

Georgetown Consortium Project published the results of its three-year language and culture learning study, which indicated students learn most effectively abroad when provided with timely, appropriate, and proactive learning interventions (Vande Berg et al. 2009), many universities began looking more seriously at how they could implement local learning or intercultural learning classes. Having had three extensive study abroad experiences myself and seen firsthand the inconsistent results of just sending students abroad without any framing for cultural learning, I began about fifteen years ago to develop courses for TCU students to improve their cultural learning while studying abroad. Despite there being a great deal of interest in the topic of intercultural courses and intervention abroad, I could not find the combination of theory and application that I was looking for to develop a syllabus. So I started with my own intercultural learning abroad, my student advising experience, and my academic grounding from a master's degree in intercultural communication and a doctorate in linguistics, and over the years have had numerous incarnations of my own intercultural learning course.

In 2010, a few colleagues on my campus were developing new study abroad programs for Honors students and asked for my help. Their newly proposed programs would be almost solely based on developing students' cultural vision, or "understanding of world cultures and cross-cultural perspectives." This interdisciplinary group of faculty had experience taking students abroad for disciplinary-specific study but was eager to focus on the cultural learning part of taking students abroad. It was the ideal group for me to test the model I'd been developing, which integrated experiential learning abroad with academic tools and structure.

Through sharing my model with TCU Honors, and in subsequent years being asked many times to share my syllabus, I have learned there is a need not just for content but also for theoretical grounding. This manual provides both academic information on intercultural learning and practical advice for helping students develop intercultural competence. It includes a summary of intercultural learning goals as well as guidance on how to achieve these goals. I describe the many valuable and wonderful resources that already exist, add some of my own, and put these in a framework to facilitate learning and growth. The result is an approach I call the PRISM: Get PREPARED, Make it RELEVANT, Get INVOLVED, Make SENSE, Make it MATTER.

Like the multifaceted object that changes the direction of light waves to produce a colorful refraction, the PRISM pedagogy changes the nature and direction of students' experiences to provide a more nuanced and vibrant understanding. Without this PRISM, studying abroad can be a superficial experience, where students see things that are intriguing or interesting but do not explore them in enough depth to understand them. The PRISM provides opportunities to change students' observations and interpretations of their experiences. It provides tools for students to uncover complexity and richness. It doesn't tell us what to see or what we'll find, but provides a different way of looking at things.

The PRISM sparks conversations, illuminates connections, and clarifies knowledge, providing students opportunities to connect and understand in intercultural contexts in ways they would otherwise miss. This book will show you, the international educator, how to use this transformational tool.

Organization and Layout of Book

This book leads you through understanding intercultural competency components, developing these components in various contexts, and creating your own application. Modeling the PRISM approach, the chapters of this book are framed around quotations to *get you prepared* and questions to *help you make it relevant*. In the first chapter, I describe some of the skills, attitudes, and knowledge that lead to intercultural competence. In the second chapter, I describe the PRISM model and approach, including the theory behind the pedagogy. In the third chapter, I provide specific, concrete examples of the PRISM learning tools that you can use in both curricular and cocurricular ways. In the appendices, I provide a sample syllabus as well as ideas for different platforms and media for utilizing the PRISM in non-classroom-based ways, from predeparture marketing and orientation to returned student celebrations and activities. The book uses study abroad experiences as the context, but the PRISM model can be applied to any intercultural learning environment.

I encourage you to adapt, modify, and expand on these ideas to make them work in your study abroad programming and intercultural learning environments. I hope the PRISM approach will spark your own ideas for encouraging students to engage in and learn from their intercultural experiences. As we all work towards deepening students' learning and engagement, PRISM can be a launching pad for a shared conversation on the development of intercultural competence.

Ultimately, the structure and tools of PRISM can help lead both educators and students to more meaningful and complex interpretations of their experiences abroad.

ACKNOWLEDGMENTS

This book could not have been possible without the assistance of many people. First, to Jane Kucko, who gave me the freedom to develop coursework at Texas Christian University (TCU) around intercultural learning and the encouragement to believe in myself and my work, thank you for your vision, collaboration, and mentorship.

To Rachel Johnston, the most amazing writing coach/editor/muse I've ever worked with, I have been privileged to have your multiple readings and edits, thoughtful feedback, and endless encouragement. You have helped me develop this work in a way I could not have done on my own. The richness of the final product is in large part thanks to you.

A very special thanks to my colleagues and graduate students who experimented with me, cotaught numerous sections, and provided invaluable feedback. In particularly, to Beata Jones, Amanda Irvin, Joanna Schmidt, and Sarah McNeeley, thank you for your enthusiasm and collaboration, particularly when I felt like giving up on this project.

To my late mother, Lynn Rundstrom: there isn't a day that goes by that I don't wish I could talk to you about many things, but most of all, to ask you how you had the courage and generosity to let me study abroad for a year at sixteen years old. The depth of that gift was profound. It set me on this most amazing path of learning about the world, and I am incredibly humbled by and grateful for that opportunity. To my brother Todd Rundstrom, for being the trailblazer who opened my eyes to the world and encouraged me to push myself beyond my comfort zone: I am beyond appreciative for your confidence in me and for your role modeling. To my father, Jim Rundstrom, who encouraged my studies abroad in spite of the fact that I seemed to have "an awful lot of once-in-a-lifetime experiences" for him to fund: I am so grateful for your support. To my sister Tammy Luna, who models intercultural competence every day in her bilingual classroom and bilingual home: I am in awe of you.

Pour vous, la famille Halbart, qui m'a accueillée dans votre maison et dans vos coeurs—je vous remercie. J'aurais bien voulu avoir un guide comme ce livre pour m'enseigner les attitudes et les comportements que j'aurais dû pratiquer. Malheureusement, vous avez dû vivre avec moi au moment où je n'avais pas ces connaissances. Les matériaux de ce livre, et la motivation pour mon texte, sont dûs presqu'exclusivement à la générosité de votre accueil. Vous êtes la raison pour laquelle je suis restée pendant toute une année, la raison que je suis devenue bilingue et bi-culturelle, et aussi la raison pour le travail en échanges d'étudiants que je fais aujourd'hui. Je vous remercie pour votre patience, votre affection, et votre générosité pendant mon développement.[1]

And most importantly to my husband Andy and sons Tristan and Spencer, who encouraged me, inspired me, and sacrificed time with me, I love you the whole world. You are my compass, my north, le sens à mes demains.

[1] For the Halbart family, who welcomed me into your home and into your hearts—thank you. I wish I could have had a guide like this book to teach me the attitudes and behaviors I needed. Unfortunately, you had to live with me when I did not have that knowledge. The materials in this book, and the motivation for my text, are almost exclusively due to the generosity of your hospitality. You are the reason I stayed for a whole year, the reason I became bilingual and bicultural, and the reason for the study abroad work that I am doing today. I thank you for your patience, your affection, and your generosity during my development.

CHAPTER 1

What Can Students Learn from Studying Abroad? Building the Theoretical Foundation for Learning Outcomes

"We go abroad not only to see different things, but to see things differently." —Anonymous

Educational Outcomes of Study Abroad Programs

As you think about what students might learn from studying abroad, it's probably not too hard to come up with ideas. There are the physical structures themselves: seeing buildings, monuments, castles, shrines, and cathedrals in contexts allows visitors to make connections and understand things through observation. For example, on my first visit to Versailles, as my jaw dropped in seeing its sheer size and opulence, my host sister said to me, "Now you see why there was a revolution. People were starving, and the king built this."

There is the natural landscape: seeing mountains, rivers, valleys, deserts, oceans, and jungles firsthand can help us make sense of how the environment has impacted, and been impacted by, the way people live their lives. For example, visiting Iquitos, Peru, a place still unconnected by road, my sister-in-law showed me the ways the Amazon River is not just a source of beauty and pride for them, but the lifeblood of their economy and their connection to the world.

And there are the people themselves, their infrastructures and systems: observing and engaging with political, social, economic, communication, art, micro and macro systems can help us not just see but also experience and understand different problems, approaches, and solutions within the shared human experience. When I take students to India to explore human trafficking, we observe and discuss the underlying matrix of poverty, population density, social immobility, and colonial legacy in ways that reading in a textbook could never bring to light.

At the root of study abroad experiences is the expectation that seeing different things leads us to see things differently. But is this always the case?

In the preceding examples, I showcase the leap from observation to deeper understanding, but students are not always able to make this leap. In fact, in each of these examples, a local person or expert provided guidance and context for interpretations. Without such guidance and context, it is almost inevitable that students will not be able to have insightful, let alone transformational, interpretations. Whether it is facilitating opportunities for students to make connections, helping them recognize what to observe or focus on, or pushing them to observe through a nonjudgmental lens, guidance is needed for growth and learning to happen.

Numerous studies confirm that merely being in another culture does not guarantee the development of new knowledge and skills. Pedersen (2010) comments that simply sending "students to a location abroad for academic study is not sufficient toward facilitating the larger goal of creating effective global citizenship" (71) and that specific learning outcomes are necessary to enhance existing programs. Hunter (2008) concludes programs will be more effective if they "do not rely on the haphazard chance of students engaging in this process [of intercultural development] on their own, but instead very intentionally organize learning activities to encourage it" (99).

But before we can begin to organize the learning activities, we need to define what it is we think students *can* and *should* learn from studying abroad. For years international educators have sought to qualify, quantify, and increase the learning that happens while studying abroad, not only to combat the stereotype that studying abroad is glorified vacation travel but to demonstrate that the outcomes achieved are significant, meaningful, and academic. These have been challenging tasks, partly because research on assessment of studying abroad has been inconsistent, but also because the learning models have often been formulated around applied and activity-oriented models that don't always seem academically grounded to faculty.

Certainly studying abroad is experiential in nature; otherwise, why change the setting of the learning environment? Clearly, the value of studying abroad comes from being in another setting and experiencing firsthand new perspectives and ways of life. And while the learning itself is applied, this is no different from any skill or competence we help students develop in traditional classroom settings on home campuses. Writing, critical thinking, and public speaking, for example, all involve learning processes that include explaining, experimenting, revising, and repeating.

Therefore, the problem is both defining and valuing the learning that can occur from studying abroad. This chapter will provide the answer—intercultural competence—and give educators the knowledge and understanding of this discipline to better assist students in developing these skills.

Intercultural Competence

As noted earlier, intercultural competence is the name given to the broad category of outcomes often expected from study abroad experiences. Intercultural competence is the knowledge, attitudes, and skills needed to be culturally appropriate and effective (Gudykunst, Ting-Toomey and Wiseman 1991, Kim 1991, Grunzweig and Rinehart 1998, Deardorff 2006, J.M. Bennett 2008).

The specific knowledge, attitudes, and skills identified by researchers as components of intercultural competence are extensive. Knowledge components have included: knowledge of the host culture (i.e., cultural and ethnic diversity, history, geography, political and economic systems, religious and spiritual beliefs, multiple value systems, and situational norms), knowledge of communication patterns and differences (i.e., language, verbal and nonverbal styles), and various problem-solving and decision-making styles. Attitudes include being flexible, open, culturally empathetic, perceptive, and nonjudgmental. Skills have included high tolerance of ambiguity, the ability to respectfully observe, creative thinking and problem-solving abilities, the ability to manage psychological stress, and cross-cultural social skills.

Deardorff's (2006, 2009) model provides structure and cohesiveness of these elements by presenting a framework for intercultural competence that draws on a consensus definition. Based on a national interdisciplinary study, the consensus definition agreed upon by leading intercultural scholars is "effective and appropriate behavior and communication in intercultural situations." From there, Deardorff

Pyramid Model of Intercultural Competence (Deardorff, 2006. 2009):

DESIRED EXTERNAL OUTCOME:

Behaving and communicating effectively and appropriately (based on one's intercultural knowledge, skills, and attitudes) to achieve one's goals to some degree

DESIRED INTERNAL OUTCOME:
Informed frame of reference/filter shift:

Adaptability (to different communication styles and behaviors; adjustment to new cultural environments);
Flexibility (selecting and using appropriate communication styles and behaviors; cognitive flexibility);
Ethnorelative view;
Empathy

Knowledge and Comprehension:

Cultural self-awareness;
Deep understanding and knowledge of culture (including contexts, role, and impact of culture and others' worldviews);
Culture-specific information;
Sociolinguistic awareness

Skills:

To listen, observe, and interpret
To analyze, evaluate, and relate

Requisite Attitudes:

Respect (valuing other cultures, cultural diversity)
Openness (to intercultural learning and to people from other cultures, withholding judgment)
Curiosity and discovery (tolerating ambiguity and uncertainty)

Notes:

- Move from personal level (attitude) to interpersonal/interactive level (outcomes)
- Degree of intercultural competence depends on acquired degree of underlying elements

identified and structured the agreed-upon essential items to create a framework of attitudes, knowledge, skills, and internal/external outcomes for intercultural competence.

The attitudes that emerged from Deardorff's study include **respect**, **openness**, and **curiosity and discovery**. The knowledge aspects identified included **cultural self-awareness**, **deep cultural knowledge** including understanding other worldviews, **culture-specific knowledge**, and **sociolinguistic awareness**. The skills that emerged from this study were ones that addressed the processing of knowledge: **observing**, **listening**, **evaluating**, **analyzing**, **interpreting**, and **relating**. It is worth mentioning the one element agreed upon by all the intercultural scholars was the importance of understanding the world from others' perspectives.

These attitudes, knowledge, and skills ideally lead to internal outcomes of **flexibility**, **adaptability**, an **ethnorelative perspective**, and **empathy**, which are then demonstrated through external actions, including **behavior** and **communication**. This leads to the agreed upon definition of intercultural competence: effective and appropriate behavior and communication in intercultural situations. This model of course recognizes that determinations of "effectiveness" and "appropriateness" are reliant on those with whom one interacts. This framework nonetheless provides both comprehensiveness and order to a set of concepts that can otherwise seem challenging to dissect and arrange.

The Association of American Colleges and Universities (AAC&U) used Deardorff's framework (along with other models and research) and published a rubric for Intercultural Knowledge and Competence, which they defined as "a set of cognitive, affective, and behavioral skills and characteristics that support effective and appropriate interaction in a variety of cultural contexts." Developed by a team of faculty experts (Bennett et al 2010) from a range of colleges and universities, the rubric articulates six learning outcomes for intercultural competence: **Cultural Self-Awareness**, **Knowledge of Cultural Worldview Frameworks**, **Empathy**, **Verbal and Non-Verbal Communication**, **Curiosity**, and **Openness;** and four performance descriptors (benchmark, milestones, and capstone) for each. These six dimensions are not necessarily comprehensive in all the aspects of intercultural knowledge and competence, but provide examples of learning outcomes that can be adapted to a course or study abroad program.

The rubric divides these six learning outcomes into cognitive elements (cultural self-awareness and knowledge of cultural worldviews), behavioral elements (empathy and verbal and non-verbal communication), and affective elements (curiosity and openness). In practice, though, it is difficult to separate them at times. As I explain each of these components below and discuss the goals for the student, you will see the ways they intertwine and draw upon each other.

Intercultural Knowledge and Competence VALUE Rubric

Association of American Colleges and Universities

For more information, please contact value@aacu.org

The VALUE rubrics were developed by teams of faculty experts representing colleges and universities across the United States through a process that examined many existing campus rubrics and related documents for each learning outcome and incorporated additional feedback from faculty. The rubrics articulate fundamental criteria for each learning outcome, with performance descriptors demonstrating progressively more sophisticated levels of attainment. The rubrics are intended for institutional-level use in evaluating and discussing student learning, not for grading. The core expectations articulated in all fifteen of the VALUE rubrics can and should be translated into the language of individual campuses, disciplines, and even courses. The utility of the VALUE rubrics is to position learning at all undergraduate levels within a basic framework of expectations such that evidence of learning can be shared nationally through a common dialogue and understanding of student success.

DEFINITION

Intercultural Knowledge and Competence is "a set of cognitive, affective, and behavioral skills and characteristics that support effective and appropriate interaction in a variety of cultural contexts." (Bennett, J. M. 2008. Transformative training: Designing programs for culture learning. In *Contemporary leadership and intercultural competence: Understanding and utilizing cultural diversity to build successful organizations*, ed. M. A. Moodian, 95-110. Thousand Oaks, CA: Sage.)

FRAMING LANGUAGE

The call to integrate intercultural knowledge and competence into the heart of education is an imperative born of seeing ourselves as members of a

Evaluators are encouraged to assign a zero to any work sample or collection of work that does not meet benchmark (cell one) level performance.

	Capstone 4	**Milestones** 3	2	**Benchmark** 1
Knowledge *Cultural self-awareness*	Articulates insights into own cultural rules and biases (e.g. seeking complexity; aware of how her/his experiences have shaped these rules, and how to recognize and respond to cultural biases, resulting in a shift in self-description.)	Recognizes new perspectives about own cultural rules and biases (e.g. not looking for sameness; comfortable with the complexities that new perspectives offer.)	Identifies own cultural rules and biases (e.g. with a strong preference for those rules shared with own cultural group and seeks the same in others.)	Shows minimal awareness of own cultural rules and biases (even those shared with own cultural group(s)) (e.g. uncomfortable with identifying possible cultural differences with others.)
Knowledge *Knowledge of cultural worldview frameworks*	Demonstrates sophisticated understanding of the complexity of elements important to members of another culture in relation to its history, values, politics, communication styles, economy, or beliefs and practices.	Demonstrates adequate understanding of the complexity of elements important to members of another culture in relation to its history, values, politics, communication styles, economy, or beliefs and practices.	Demonstrates partial understanding of the complexity of elements important to members of another culture in relation to its history, values, politics, communication styles, economy, or beliefs and practices.	Demonstrates surface understanding of the complexity of elements important to members of another culture in relation to its history, values, politics, communication styles, economy, or beliefs and practices.
Skills *Empathy*	Interprets intercultural experience from the perspectives of own and more than one worldview and demonstrates ability to act in a supportive manner that recognizes the feelings of another cultural group.	Recognizes intellectual and emotional dimensions of more than one worldview and sometimes uses more than one worldview in interactions.	Identifies components of other cultural perspectives but responds in all situations with own worldview.	Views the experience of others but does so through own cultural worldview.

Skills *Verbal and nonverbal communication*	Articulates a complex understanding of cultural differences in verbal and nonverbal communication (e.g., demonstrates understanding of the degree to which people use physical contact while communicating in different cultures or use direct/indirect and explicit/implicit meanings) and is able to skillfully negotiate a shared understanding based on those differences.	Recognizes and participates in cultural differences in verbal and nonverbal communication and begins to negotiate a shared understanding based on those differences.	Identifies some cultural differences in verbal and nonverbal communication and is aware that misunderstandings can occur based on those differences but is still unable to negotiate a shared understanding.	Has a minimal level of understanding of cultural differences in verbal and nonverbal communication; is unable to negotiate a shared understanding.
Attitudes *Curiosity*	Asks complex questions about other cultures, seeks out and articulates answers to these questions that reflect multiple cultural perspectives.	Asks deeper questions about other cultures and seeks out answers to these questions.	Asks simple or surface questions about other cultures.	States minimal interest in learning more about other cultures.
Attitudes *Openness*	Initiates and develops interactions with culturally different others. Suspends judgment in valuing her/his interactions with culturally different others.	Begins to initiate and develop interactions with culturally different others. Begins to suspend judgment in valuing her/his interactions with culturally different others.	Expresses openness to most, if not all, interactions with culturally different others. Has difficulty suspending any judgment in her/his interactions with culturally different others, and is aware of own judgment and expresses a willingness to change.	Receptive to interacting with culturally different others. Has difficulty suspending any judgment in her/his interactions with culturally different others, but is unaware of own judgment.

world community, knowing that we share the future with others. Beyond mere exposure to culturally different others, the campus community requires the capacity to: meaningfully engage those others, place social justice in historical and political context, and put culture at the core of transformative learning. The intercultural knowledge and competence rubric suggests a systematic way to measure our capacity to identify our own cultural patterns, compare and contrast them with others, and adapt empathically and flexibly to unfamiliar ways of being.

The levels of this rubric are informed in part by M. Bennett's Developmental Model of Intercultural Sensitivity (Bennett, M.J. 1993. Towards ethnorelativism: A developmental model of intercultural sensitivity. In *Education for the intercultural experience*, ed. R. M. Paige, 22-71. Yarmouth, ME: Intercultural Press). In addition, the criteria in this rubric are informed in part by D.K. Deardorff's intercultural framework which is the first research-based consensus model of intercultural competence (Deardorff, D.K. 2006. The identification and assessment of intercultural competence as a student outcome of internationalization. *Journal of Studies in International Education* 10(3): 241-266). It is also important to understand that intercultural knowledge and competence is more complex than what is reflected in this rubric. This rubric identifies six of the key components of intercultural knowledge and competence, but there are other components as identified in the Deardorff model and in other research.

GLOSSARY

The definitions that follow were developed to clarify terms and concepts used in this rubric only.

- Culture: All knowledge and values shared by a group.
- Cultural rules and biases: Boundaries within which an individual operates in order to feel a sense of belonging to a society or group, based on the values shared by that society or group.
- Empathy: "Empathy is the imaginary participation in another person's experience, including emotional and intellectual dimensions, by imagining his or her perspective (not by assuming the person's position)." Bennett, J. 1998.
- Transition shock: Putting culture shock in perspective. In *Basic concepts of intercultural communication*, ed. M. Bennett, 215-224. Yarmouth, ME: Intercultural Press.
- Intercultural experience: The experience of an interaction with an individual or groups of people whose culture is different from your own.
- Intercultural/cultural differences: The differences in rules, behaviors,

- communication and biases, based on cultural values that are different from one's own culture.
- Suspending judgment in valuing their interactions with culturally different others: Postponing assessment or evaluation (positive or negative) of interactions with people culturally different from oneself. Disconnecting from the process of automatic judgment and taking time to reflect on possibly multiple meanings.
- Worldview: The cognitive and affective lens through which people construe their experiences and make sense of the world around them.

The components from Deardorff's model and the AAC&U rubric can serve as a starting point for developing a framework for intercultural learning, and in the following pages I will describe these concepts further, giving an explanation for each as well as some broad suggestions for helping your students understand and apply the concepts.

Cultural Self-Awareness

Cultural self-awareness is recognizing that many of the aspects of who we are, what we believe, and how we behave have been taught to us, and that they are not the only or the right way of being in the world. Cultural self-awareness means moving beyond ethnocentrism, or the belief that one's culture is the center of the world and has the only or best way of doing things. Without cultural self-awareness, it is easy to judge others. You may believe that everyone should think and act and believe the way you do, because you have not been exposed to other ways of thinking and acting and believing. This is very understandable, because this is how a culture works. You are surrounded by people who think and act in similar ways, and they unconsciously reinforce those thoughts and behaviors.

Our culture is reinforced both in the places and in the customs we inhabit. In English, the word "inhabit" conveys that we live, dwell, or reside in a particular location or place. At the root is "habit," which is useful in becoming more aware that in our own cultural homes, we are living inside customs, routines, practices, traditions, and patterns—or habits.

Cultural self-awareness learning may include identifying specific aspects of one's culture, such as "Americans are time-oriented," or simply recognizing that we have a culture, and that many of the behaviors, values, and attitudes we have are not universal or "normal," but actually socialized ways of being in the world.

Understanding our individual cultures is the first step in overcoming the influences that impede our ability to engage with others. Cultural self-awareness is important in intercultural learning because before you can understand another, you need to understand yourself. To understand others, you must first realize the influence of your own culture on your values and thinking. Only then can you come to value other ways of thinking and being in the world.

A cultural self-awareness mindset brings attention to the interpretations we make and biases we have about what we see. "We all believe that we observe reality—things as they are. But what actually happens is that the mind interprets what the eye sees and gives it meaning. It is only at this point, when meaning is assigned, that we can truly say we have *seen* something. In other words, what we see is as much in the mind as it is in reality" (Peace Corps 2002, 29 – 30).

Because culture is by definition unconscious and ingrained, it can be difficult to identify one's own culture. Assuming your students are US Americans, an insightful explanation of US American culture is L. Robert Kohls's "Values Americans Live By" (1984):

1. Personal Control over the Environment: We believe we have the right to alter nature for our own purposes and to exert control over the natural world to the extent we are able; fate is in our hands.
2. Change Is Good: Change is good and is associated with progress and improvement and is considered essential to development.
3. Time and Its Control Are Important: Time is considered an important commodity and needs to be used wisely, leading to emphasis on time management and adhering to schedules.

4. Equality and Egalitarianism: There is a central belief in the basic equality of opportunity for human beings and equal protection under the law, as well as equal social treatment.
5. Individualism and Privacy: Each person is considered a unique individual and a high value is placed on personal style and action. Privacy is valued as necessary to one's self and is often jealously protected against intrusions.
6. Self-help: Accomplishment is based upon what one does for oneself, and getting ahead requires individual effort.
7. Competition and Free Enterprise: Competition is viewed as natural and positive and free enterprise is the preferred economic system to facilitate this process.
8. Future Orientation: Belief that "the best is yet to come" makes Americans stress the future rather than the past or present; we generally have optimistic expectations.
9. Action/Work Orientation: Active engagement and planning is seen as useful. "Don't just stand there, do something" is a basic American attitude. One's identity is derived significantly from what one does for a living. Busy is good.
10. Informality: Emphasis is on a casual approach to many things including social interactions, clothes, and communication styles.
11. Directness, Openness, Honesty: Sincerity is thought to be demonstrated by the degree of open and frank discussion involved. Honesty is equated with a certain bluntness and directness. Little ritualism is tolerated and "telling it like it is" is admired.
12. Practicality and Efficiency: "What works" is valued, realistic assessments preferred to philosophic speculations, and making things "better" and "faster" is applauded.
13. Materialism and Acquisitiveness: Acquiring goods and services is a natural reward for hard work, and doing so is seen as a reasonable goal.

As you examine these with students, you may find that they (and perhaps you) find it nearly impossible to think that anyone would *not* value these. This is case in point what culture does: it conditions us to think and behave in ways that ultimately become so ingrained and unconscious that we take them to be universal. Take, for example, the notion of efficiency, which underlies everything from our approach to service at restaurants to our use of technology. We can sometimes find there is another value at play when we don't see efficiency in other cultures, such as valuing enjoyment of conversation and food at restaurants over fast service. But there are other situations where we may be just flat-out baffled at processes that seem so antithetical to efficiency, such as when a hotel worker rewrites a complete form by hand rather than use the copy machine. It may be that there is indeed a rationale or purpose, or it may be that efficiency is simply not even considered.

Simply being in another culture can bring awareness of our own culture, but does not guarantee we will think in deep and meaningful ways about our own culture. In some cases, being in another culture may cause us to be critical of people in that culture and defensive of our own culture. This is why the intentionality of the PRISM program is helpful in moving students toward higher levels of cultural self-awareness.

Ethnorelative Understanding of Cultural Worldviews

A worldview is "the cognitive and affective lens through which people construe their experiences and make sense of the world around them" (Association of American Colleges and Universities 2009). Cultures have shared worldviews because the people within the culture share a history, language, set of values, and common experiences that unite and influence and motivate them. To develop an understanding of other cultural worldviews, we must appreciate the elements that shape others' construction of their experiences and respect their viewpoints without judgment. It does not require us to adopt another culture's beliefs and values as our own, but rather strive to understand where they come from, which may include historical, political, economic, environmental, religious, and social factors, and to validate that these beliefs and values are rational and meaningful to others.

To do so, we can start by understanding how we are enculturated. Different models or metaphors have been used to describe culture, which can be instructive in helping students gain an understanding of cultural worldviews. Anthropologist Edward Hall (1976) describes culture as having both

Iceberg Concept of Culture

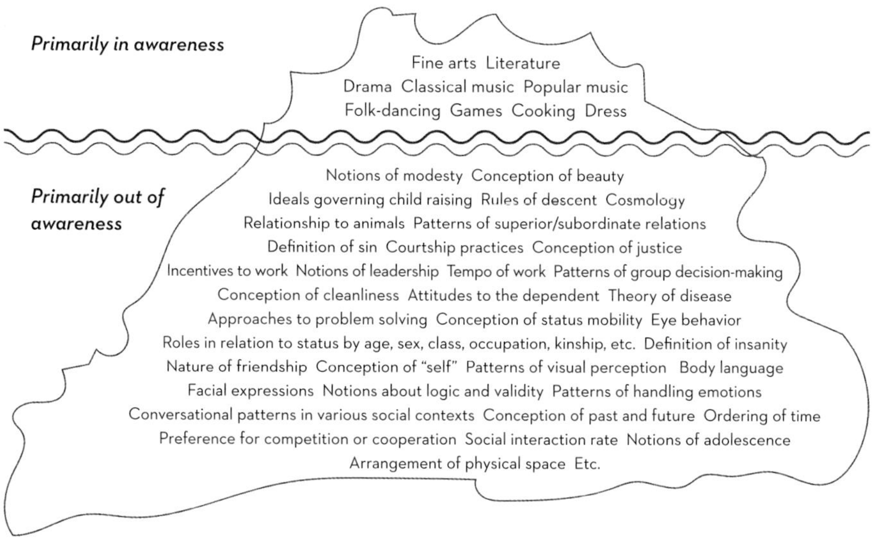

Source: p. 14 AFS Orientation Handbook Vol. 4 New York: AFS Intercultural Programs Inc., 1984
Reprinted with permission from AFS.

surface and deep layers, writing "beneath the clearly perceived, highly explicit surface culture there lies a whole other world, which when understood will ultimately radically change our view of human nature" (15). This has led to culture sometimes being described as an iceberg, where the surface, or visible culture, such as behaviors, mannerisms, and expressions is built on the deep, or invisible culture, which are the beliefs, values, and thought patterns. When we first encounter a culture, only the most overt behaviors are apparent, but as we spend more time in a culture, we can uncover the underlying, unconscious patterns that drive the conscious, visible culture. The iceberg metaphor can be used to show students why they should not judge a culture based solely on the visible piece and instead take time to uncover underlying values and beliefs. It also reminds us that for everyone, those within and those outside a culture, the visible parts of culture are the easiest to identify, but the invisible parts of culture, which are much harder to identify, are also more influential.

Another approach for teaching awareness of cultural frameworks is Hofstede's model of influences or mental programming (1980, 2001).

Hofstede says our behaviors and perceptions are influenced by three components: human nature, culture, and personality:

Levels of Influences (Hofstede 2001)

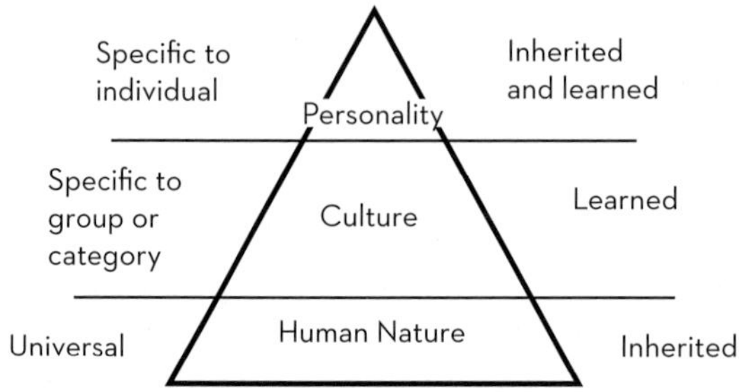

Copyright 2001 by Geert Hofstede B. V. reprinted with permission

The deepest level, human nature, describes our biological influences, such as hunger, territoriality, and nurturing offspring. Placed at the base of the pyramid, this represents the core set of influences shared by all members of the human race regardless of their culture, which sometimes leads people to say things like, "we're all really the same inside." At the other end, the tip of the pyramid, is the shallowest level, personality, or those unique aspects of our genetic makeup and personal experiences that lead to our personal perceptions and behaviors which make us different from others, even those of the same culture. In this model, the level or influence of personality is far less than the other two, but still important.

The middle level, culture, refers to the influence of our taught social experience. In this model, our culture trains us on how to interpret our environs and how to behave to get what is needed from the environment. Unlike human nature, which is inherited, and personality, which is both inherited and learned, culture is learned: acquired from other members of our cultural group through direct instructions (as to children), observation, and reinforcement. But, once acquired, it becomes an automatic way of interacting and understanding one another and the world, and a subconscious influence on our actions. As we saw in cultural self-awareness, most people are not aware of their culture;

it is simply what they think of as normal behavior. We are a part of many different cultures that influence us, including gender, religion, age, interest group, and of course nationality. According to Hofstede, all of these influences—human nature, culture, and personality—blend together, making us multifaceted, complex beings who have both commonalities with and differences from all of the other multifaceted, complex beings in the world.

Embedded in both of these models is an understanding that cultures are taught and acquired, and not intrinsically right or wrong—just different from one another. They are a society's interpretation of appropriateness. Being able to see another culture's worldview in a nonjudgmental way is called ethnorelativism, and we should push our students to gain this ethnorelative perspective. An ethnorelative perspective means acknowledging the cultural behaviors and beliefs of others are as valid, logical, and appropriate as one's own.

These models can provide frameworks for understanding culture as a phenomenon and for appreciating the cultural worldviews of others we encounter. An intentional approach to exploring cultural worldviews is essential, because, while simply being in another culture can expose us to other worldviews, it does not guarantee we understand those worldviews or respect them with an ethnorelative perspective. In fact, without conversation and contextualization, we can remain superficial and judgmental of others.

It is for this reason that we must actively and intentionally push students to dig deeper, examine more thoroughly, and explore more openly to move them to *more ethnorelative understanding of cultural worldviews.*

Culture-Specific Knowledge

When students say they want to learn about another culture, they typically mean they want to gain culture-specific knowledge. Without intentionality, though, mere encounters with others of another culture does not always lead to culture-specific knowledge. Students may focus on superficial differences and make broad generalizations, often without critical thinking or analysis. Students may also fail to distinguish between cultural influences and personality differences.

While closely integrated with ethnorelative understanding of cultural worldview, gaining culture-specific knowledge is less theoretical and more practical. Developing culture-specific knowledge involves learning about elements of another culture, such as history, politics, communication styles, economy, practices, and beliefs, as well as the relevance of each. One approach to gaining culture-specific knowledge is ethnographic study. Ethnographic study typically involves a "detailed, in-depth description of everyday life and practice" (Hoey 2014, 1) that comes from living among a different cultural group. Ethnographers generate understandings of culture using an emic perspective or "insider's point of view." The ethnographer does not simply report events and observations but attempts to explain how these represent what we might call "webs of meaning" (Geertz).

To help students think about how to explain and interpret their observations, the following from Hoey may be helpful:

What Sort of Questions Do Ethnographers Ask Themselves?

1. Who are key actors in a given context?
2. What happens in a given place and time? What catches your attention? Often we tend to notice what seems "unusual" or "different." That's why working in another culture from our own can be helpful. We tend to notice those things with which we are not familiar. . . . What markers of identity are there in this group or at this place? Would the people with whom you are working recognize these markers themselves or does it take an "outsider" to see them as such?
3. Where do you find the subjects of your study, i.e., the people from whom you are learning? What does this place look like? What does it sound like? Basically, what are your sensory impressions of this place?
4. When do things happen? Do they always happen at this time? Again, we're looking for suggestive patterns. So do any behaviors, events, or utterances seem to follow a certain order? Are there any nonverbal

cues or body language that prompt people to take action in a given situation according to what appears to be some prearrangement or understanding?

5. How do things appear to work? That is, are there written rules that people follow? Are there tacit understandings? How do people know how to behave? Is it always the same? Do different "categories" of persons behave differently—young or old, "black" or "white," male or female, newcomer or oldhand?
6. Gradually, as you work through the nuts and bolts, you can begin to think about the larger questions. You start doing this early on because (again) you're trying to develop an understanding. You will need to continue to refine this understanding but start asking things like: Why did this thing happen? (Hoey 2014, 6 – 7).

As with ethnorelative understanding of cultural worldviews, developing culture-specific knowledge should incorporate a nonjudgmental perspective. Despite good intentions, it can be challenging to avoid interpreting from one's own perspective. For many first-time ethnographers, being judgmental or comparative about differences is hard to avoid. For this reason, it is important to provide feedback and guidance to students about how to make interpretations based on observations.

In addition to observing and interpreting daily behavior and events through ethnography, it is also important to learn about the structural and contextual components that influence people's culture. This includes learning about the history, economy, political structures and influences, language, and collective memory and lore. Undoubtedly, this is a tall order. It may make more sense to students to look for readings, videos, and materials that help them make the connection between this information and its influence on current life. Consider documentaries and stories from public radio and public television.

As you help students gain culture-specific knowledge, it is important to recognize the complexity of cultural—and personality—influences on each person, as well as the diversity of individuals in any one culture. Gaining culture-specific knowledge means moving beyond simple and sweeping generalizations about a group of people, what Adichie calls the *single story*: "There is danger in a single story. The single story creates stereotypes, and the problem with stereotypes is not that they are untrue, but they are incomplete" (2009). For more *complete* understanding, we must work to delve into deeper understandings of people as both individuals and products of their culture.

Simply being in another culture can bring awareness of certain aspects of culture, but it does not guarantee we will recognize the complexity and richness of a culture and its individual people. For example, I can spend time in India and notice the food is spicy and the style of dress is more modest, and still not have any sense of the historical, environmental, and religious influences on food and dress, such as regional and religious influences on food or the intersections of class and religion on styles of dress. However, with intentionality and focus, students can develop *culture-specific knowledge* that will increase their intercultural competence.

Empathy and Respect

Empathy is the ability to see experiences from more than one worldview and to behave in a manner that takes into account the feelings of others. This is particularly relevant when cultural influences may lead someone to have feelings that are different from what you would feel.

In its most basic sense, empathy is "our ability to identify what someone else is thinking and feeling and to respond to their thoughts and feelings with an appropriate emotion" (Baron-Cohen 2011, 16). It is different from sympathy or feeling sadness for someone else; rather, it is vicariously experiencing the feelings, perceptions and thoughts of another. Empathy is largely a part of our human experience, as we are soft-wired for sociability, attachment, affection, and companionship. We long to connect with others and to belong. It is this drive to connect with others and to belong that pushes us to try to understand and experience others' feelings, to empathize (Pederson & Pope 2010, Rifkin 2010).

Being empathetic means both recognizing and responding to other people's feelings and reactions. Simply recognizing is not enough; responding to and/or considering how something will make others feel and how it impacts others is necessary, too (Baron-Cohen 2011). "Empathy leads us not only to experience the feelings of another but also to reflect on those feelings and compare them to our own" (Zhu 2011, 117).

Honing empathy in intercultural settings requires work for several reasons. First, we need to see culturally different others as part of our community. While we have a human drive to empathize, it can be limited to those we think we are most like: often those with whom we share a language, religion, race, or nationality. Developing empathy across the human race requires a shift in our thinking, from seeing people who look, speak, and act differently as "others" to seeing them as "like us" (Rifkin 2010).

Second, intercultural empathy requires us to recognize that "the same behaviors may have different meanings and that different behaviors may have the same meanings" across cultures (Pedersen and Pope 2010, 848). Our sense of what constitutes polite or impolite behavior, kindness or disrespect, often come from our culture, and thus our resulting feelings are often culturally bound. For example, a direct imperative like "Pass me the salt" can be seen as a sign of closeness in Spain while it can be considered a sign of hierarchy or disrespect in the US. In intercultural situations, we have to not only recognize but empathize with others' feelings even when those feelings seem counter to ours or do not immediately make sense.

Finally, we need to recognize that culture can influence what kinds of responses are appropriate to behaviors, such as greetings, jokes, misconduct, or bodily functions, to name a few. What is considered an appropriate reaction in one culture may be inappropriate in another. Developing intercultural empathy means we must recognize that the other's thoughts and feelings reflect a different worldview and value set, and we must try to respond to others in a manner appropriate for their culture. For instance, while in Japan I might be eating on a train or while walking and find people staring at me, and think they are staring because I am a foreigner. If I realize that they are staring because I am being impolite by eating in a shared space and being messy, offering a loud and self-deprecating apology may only cause them further discomfort if they expect an honorific apology or quiet cleaning up of the space. Developing intercultural empathy means understanding what causes others to feel embarrassed, uncomfortable, and angry *as well as* recognizing how to respond to those reactions. As such, empathy builds on understanding of cultural worldviews and culture-specific knowledge, and reinforces the idea that different cultures have different behaviors, values and expectations.

Intercultural empathy may test our own feelings and reactions because it is not easy to see from another perspective. Our default is to judge from our own perspective. The ability to understand from another's perspectives requires humility and an ability to give up being "right." It requires carefully listening to others rather than being defensive or feeling threatened by others' beliefs. Developing intercultural empathy often means recognizing our biases and welcoming new perspectives and viewpoints.

While developing intercultural empathy requires opening up and trying to understand another's perspective, it does not mean having to internalize or adopt the other's perspective. We do not have to completely agree with others' values and beliefs to understand them, and we do not have to be like someone of another culture to have empathy. Rather, empathy is being mindful of the thoughts and feelings of others, respectfully acknowledging others' perspectives, and meeting shared problems by engaging with others. Students do not need to espouse others' habits, values, and beliefs, but they do need to understand that these are meaningful and valuable and logical to others.

Providing students with stories or analogies is a strategy to help students understand another's perspective. Stories and analogies can help students more easily process experiences, relate to emotions, understand rationales, and put themselves in other people's shoes (Suthakaran 2011, 208). For some ideas, see the many stories, personal essays, and folktales from Peace Corps Volunteers, http://www.peacecorps.gov/wws/stories/. One of my personal favorites, "A Single, Lucid Moment," http://www.peacecorps.gov/wws/stories/single-lucid-moment/, describes a Peace Corps Volunteer working with villagers in a rural tribe in Papua New Guinea. The villagers notice a homeless man in one of his photos from home and offer solutions to help. Examining this story with students provides an opportunity to explore multiple perspectives, identify the values and assumptions underlying varying perspectives, and empathize with the resulting feelings and interpretations.

Through this approach and the components of the PRISM program, you can help move your students to deeper levels of *empathy and respect.*

Sociolinguistic Awareness and Intercultural Communication Skills

Communication is the process of using verbal and nonverbal components to share meaning. These verbal and nonverbal components include words, grammar, intonation, volume, directness, eye contact, physical touch, facial expressions, gestures, and more. Communication is successful when people have shared interpretations of the verbal and nonverbal components used.

Culture often provides the framework for people to share meanings; we learn meanings for verbal and nonverbal components through instruction and interaction with other members in our culture. We may learn it explicitly, for example, when a parent tells a child, "Say please," or implicitly, such as when we recognize we upset or offended someone and learn how to adjust our verbal and nonverbal components to get a better result. Our sociolinguistic awareness, or ability to use communication elements appropriately, thus becomes finely tuned in our own culture.

Like our cultural norms, our interpreted meanings for different verbal and nonverbal components become so habitual and familiar that we do not think about or question them. We tend to take communication for granted and assume others have the same meanings and intentions as we do, but that is not always the case, particularly when we cross cultures. When people of different cultures try to communicate, they may have different meanings for the verbal and nonverbal components used, leading to misunderstandings. We do not always process misunderstandings consciously or rationally, though. Rather, we may blame the other for sending an unclear message, or we assume the other intended the meaning we received and take offense. On the flip side, we often assume that everything we say is understood in the way we mean it. If someone does not understand us, we think they are incompetent or uncooperative. This blaming and labeling of the other is seen when we feel irritation and anger, or when we display behaviors and reactions such as speaking louder or slower, rolling our eyes, and sighing.

Developing sociolinguistic awareness and intercultural communication skills involves recognizing that there may be different meanings associated with the same verbal and nonverbal components and that the meaning we take may not be the meaning intended. Alternatively, we may encounter new verbal and nonverbal components that require "decoding" to learn their intended meanings. Effective intercultural communicators seek to identify these different practices and meanings and adapt to them.

Examining our meanings and looking for new ones takes effort and patience. It involves interrupting our rote reactions and being observant and aware. Approaches to learning new meanings can be both overt (asking and verifying) or covert (observing and imitating). Often, though, it takes being able to dissect a communication event into its components in order to uncover the sociolinguistic differences. Communication components can include nonverbal aspects such as gestures, postures, and eye contact; phonetic aspects such as tone, volume, and speed; lexical aspects or word choices; grammatical aspects; and pragmatic aspects such as contextual meaning, turn-taking, and pacing of the conversation. As an example, we could use this approach in a restaurant scenario where we feel we are not getting the service we want and we might uncover the following. First, we could look at the nonverbals being used. What is the meaning each of us intend with our hand gestures and eye contact, and do they differ? Is something I intend as friendly interpreted as an insult? Second, we could examine phonetic pieces. Is the rising intonation I am using to ask a question interpreted as sarcasm? Third, we might look at the semantic aspects. What words am I using that might have different interpretations from what I intended? Finally, I can examine the pragmatic or contextual aspects. For example, are there different interactional patterns for customer service we should use in this culture?

The exercise on the following page demonstrates how to do this in depth and provides examples of differences on each of these four levels of communication.

Once a communicative event is broken down into components, like the MEANing components below, individuals can discuss what meaning they derive from each component. For example, one individual may report they find interrupting indicates disrespect or lack of listening, while another individual may report it means engaged listening. Or, one individual may indicate that using direct grammar indicates they feel close to the other person and don't have to bother with niceties, while another individual may indicate that it signals rudeness. Through practice and awareness, the competent intercultural communicator can identify cultural differences in order to understand others and apply different norms to appropriately convey messages.

The MEANing categories are not mutually exclusive; often they bleed into one another. However, this can help students begin to have some organizing tools and language to describe their new *intercultural communication* interactions and improve their *sociolinguistic awareness*.

Curiosity and Discovery

Curiosity is an essential component of intercultural competence, encouraging us to seek out information about our new environs and to strive to understand more deeply and completely. Curious people explore beyond the limitations of their knowledge, seek out the unfamiliar, and embrace uncertainty. While this is uncomfortable for many of us, being uncomfortable often leads to profound learning experiences and incredible growth.

To be curious is to question or *quest* for more: more understanding, more connection, more meaning. To question means to embrace our lack of knowledge and our vulnerabilities, which is not easy to do, not just

What do they MEAN?

Divide communication into its parts to add up the meaning

	Consider the communication parts	Explore the meaning
Moves (Pragmatics)	Who initiates the conversation? How do they initiate it? How does turn-taking occur? Are there any interruptions? How are they handled? How is the conversation ended?	What is my interpretation of each of these moves? Could the speaker have a different intention?
Elements (Grammar choices, word choices)	What words or expressions are chosen? Are they formal, casual, or colloquial? What grammar and structures are used (i.e., questions, orders, statements)? Is the language direct or indirect?	What is my interpretation of each of these word and grammar choices? Could the speaker have a different intention?
Audibles (Tone, inflection, sounds)	What is the tone used? How are stress, volume, inflections, and accent used? What other utterances are heard?	What is my interpretation of each of these audibles? Could the speaker have a different intention?
Nonverbals	What gestures and facial expressions are used? What body language, touch, and special movements are used?	What is my interpretation of each of these nonverbals? Could the speaker have a different intention?

because it may feel unsettling or uncomfortable. US society encourages us to be "certain and decisive, to find firm answers to questions, to seek closure, and when possible, to avoid ambiguity and the tension it brings" (Kashdan 2009, 24). Unfortunately, this stops the learning process and the possibility for growth.

> We often end up shutting down our search for information too early in the process. In essence, we become close-minded. We protect our beliefs even when they might be wrong. If someone shares our views, we praise them; if someone questions or challenges our views, we criticize, attack, and discount them (Kashdan 2009, 24).

To increase our knowledge and our connections with others we must seek out the unknown and the unfamiliar, and we must embrace questioning.

One way to develop the characteristic of curiosity is to cultivate a sense of wonder, as in "I wonder why this is here? I wonder what this is for? I wonder what else this means?" Our default mode of thinking is mindlessness, where we reflexively label and categorize things. Mindlessness serves us well in everyday life because it conserves mental energy, but it closes down the process of learning. Because mindlessness is unconscious and instinctive, we have to actively interrupt this process and initiate mindfulness and questioning, especially in ways that elicit stories and connection with others. As educators we must encourage students to ask questions, especially questions that move beyond a yes or no answer. These kinds of questions lead to stories and insight about the experiences and perspectives of others. I even suggest asking the same question of different people and asking questions I think I know the answer to in order to keep exploring perspectives and nuance. For example, if there is an election occurring in a country I am visiting, I may ask cab drivers, hotel staff, and tour guides what issues are central to the debate; if I see a festival or event taking place, I'll ask people about its history, significance, and current practices or customs.

We can build students' curiosity by creating environments where uncertainty is welcome, where it is safe to make mistakes and to admit ignorance. Wesch encourages professors and students to change our focus from being “knowledgeable to knowledge-able” (2009). In other words, instead of focusing on what you know, focus on your ability to learn and know more. Many of us are afraid to show what we do not know or understand, but not knowing is not a flaw. The flaw, according to Wesch, is not wanting to know more. Having a curious attitude means students are knowledge-able, or able to learn more.

To do this, Wesch (2009) suggests “not teaching subjects but subjectivities: ways of approaching, understanding, and interacting with the world.” For example, rather than teaching the “subject” of intercultural learning, you can encourage the following subjectivities for your students while they are abroad:

- Don’t assume sameness
- Remember that what you think of as normal or human behavior may only be cultural; what you think is common sense is really cultural sense.
- Recognize familiar behaviors may have different meanings
- Don’t assume what you meant is what was understood
- Don’t assume what you understood is what was meant
- Seek to uncover and understand: most people behave rationally; you just need to find their rationale (adapted from Stori 1994, 129-132).

These subjectivities can almost become mantras for interrupting the reflexive categorization and labeling process of mindlessness. Teach students to first recognize a categorization or judgmental thought, and when those thoughts arise, to interrupt the mindless process with one of the above subjectivities, and use that as a launching pad to ask questions.

Many people also worry about how to frame questions so that they do not come across as intrusive or judgmental. The best way to do this is to start with intentions: if your intentions are to seek out genuine connection and understanding, most people will respond positively. Model ways students can ask questions. For some, they may move through a process of observing a difference, reading or researching it, and then asking someone about it. Others may feel more comfortable asking people directly after observing something of interest.

As they begin to piece together their new insights, you should also remind students that every individual they meet is unique and complex, and the insights students learn may reflect any part of that individual, from their personality to their regional, religious, professional, socio-economic, or, of course, national culture. As long as they are continuing to seek out information, though, you should see students begin to increase their *curiosity*.

Openness and Flexibility

While being abroad, we want students to engage with others in non-judgmental ways, practice new behaviors, and stretch beyond their comfort zone. This requires openness and flexibility. With openness, students explore differences and possibilities without being derogatory or defensive about other habits, behaviors, values, and beliefs. Openness requires flexibility—to engage with different people, to experiment, and to be comfortable with mistakes. In fact, one of the predictors of success in intercultural situations is the ability to deal with rejection and failure.

To foster the capacity for openness and flexibility, encourage students to focus on their efforts rather than their abilities. When students focus on abilities, such as being smart or talented, they may resist trying something new if it threatens their sense of their abilities, such as making them appear *not* smart or *not* talented. If, on the other hand, students are praised for their efforts (to try, to learn, to work hard), they attach worth to the effort rather than the outcome. They become excited about the process of trying and exploring and develop an openness to learning (Dweck 2006).

A great mantra for openness is "becoming is better than being" (Dweck 25, 2006). When you think of yourself in "being" terms, you are focused on what you have already accomplished. "Being" categorizations are typically limited to things you have done for a long time and feel very confident about (as in, "I am a tennis player"), which can certainly be noteworthy, but also keeps you stagnant. "Becoming" categorizations are a way of branding yourself or your students as growing, learning, and working toward something, in a way that is not threatening but in fact inspiring. You can ask them their goals, and then encourage them to use these as "becoming" self-identifiers, as in, "I'm becoming a French speaker," "I'm becoming knowledgeable about healthcare in the UK," "I'm becoming an activist on social injustice in India." Each opportunity abroad provides them another chance to fulfill that statement.

The test of openness is not only seen in the ways students grow their own skill sets, but also in the ways they interact with others abroad. One measure of openness is students initiating interactions and engaging with others in nonjudgmental and cooperative ways. Students should challenge themselves to move outside their comfort zone to meet and interact with new people. No doubt this may come more easily for extroverted students or students who think on their feet. Students who are more introverted may find it helpful to have a mental bank of questions for approaching and interacting with people. Remind students that they can ask different people the same question, as this helps them piece together different perspectives within another culture and uncover deeper understandings.

To practice and develop the skill sets of openness, consider using improvisation strategies or exercises. Improvisation puts people in a situation of reacting to unexpected situations in a nonjudgmental, cooperative way. Spolin (1986) suggests improvisational theatre exercises as curricular supplements to increase students' communication and social skills, spontaneity, inventive problem solving, and creativity. Students can practice improvisation to develop flexibility and openness, along with empathy (as they watch each other struggle) and graciousness (as they find ways to help each other). If actually practicing improv seems too intimidating, simply reviewing the key techniques can provide helpful advice to students. Some core techniques of improvisation include:

Say "yes," which doesn't mean following blindly, but finding a way to keep an open mind. Listen in order to receive.

> **Say "yes *and*,"** which means finding something positive to contribute, and receiving others' recommendations without judgment. Build on what you receive.
>
> **Go with the flow**, which means taking advantage of what you see around you and making the best of every situation you find yourself in. Let go of your agenda and keep moving forward. (Flanagan 2015).

Knowing how far to push students outside their comfort zone is tricky. For most people, interacting when there is uncertainty or ambiguity causes stress, but these situations are often where the most learning takes place. In his foundational work on student development, Sanford (1962) discusses the "challenge/support balance." His theory states that for growth and personal development to occur, a person needs a balanced amount of challenge and support appropriate for the task. With too much support and/or not enough challenge, students will not learn what they need to grow and develop, but with too much challenge and/or not enough support, students will be frustrated and overwhelmed and be unable to learn. Finding the optimal level of challenge depends on the individual, but the important point is that students should be challenged to interact outside their personal comfort zones.

One of the byproducts of openness is emotional resilience, or the ability to respond to disappointment, mistakes, or failure. "An appropriate degree of challenge will create some degree of failure" (Guadagnoli et al 2012, 451) but will also lead to learning and to future success. It is important for students to be told that mistakes are not only a natural byproduct of trying new things, they are instructive as well. Haidt states, "People need adversity, setbacks, and perhaps even trauma to reach the highest levels of strength, fulfillment, and personal development" (2006:136). Being open to new cultural experiences and understandings may result in embarrassment, mistakes, confusion, or frustration, but will also lead to new understandings, skill sets, and personal growth.

As students learn to experiment with new behaviors and seek out interactions with culturally different others, they can increase their *openness, flexibility,* and emotional resilience.

Conclusion

Understanding these components of intercultural competence can help you facilitate students' development of the knowledge, skills, and attitudes needed to be culturally appropriate and effective. These components are just one way to delineate intercultural competence, and even after defining the components, there are numerous ways to organize them.

To turn these components into learning goals for your students, you could develop a learning outcome for each of the components, such as:

1. Students will articulate insights into their own cultural rules and biases (**Cultural Self-Knowledge**).
2. Students will identify the cultural elements that underlie and shape the viewpoints of others and respect them without judgment (**Ethnorelative Understanding of Cultural Worldviews).**
3. Students will articulate specific values, habits, norms, and their significance, typical of members of another culture (**Culture-Specific Knowledge**).
4. Student will demonstrate an ability to interpret intercultural experience from more than one worldview and an ability to act in a supportive manner that recognizes the feelings of culturally different others (**Empathy and Respect**).
5. Students will articulate an understanding of cultural differences in verbal and nonverbal communication and be able to skillfully negotiate a shared understanding based on those differences (**Sociolinguistic Awareness and Intercultural Communication Skills**).
6. Students will demonstrate an ability to ask complex questions about other cultures and seek out answers to these questions that reflect multiple cultural perspectives (**Curiosity and Discovery**).
7. Students will demonstrate an ability to seek out interactions with different people and practice new, culturally appropriate behaviors (**Openness and Flexibility**).

Or you could identify some conceptual constructs (for example, cultural self-awareness, awareness of other cultures, and communication differences), and move students through understanding them (knowledge) to valuing them (promoting empathy and openness) and acting on them (promoting skills). For example:

1. Students will demonstrate **cultural self-awareness**: an understanding of cultural norms and values specific to their own culture, an ability to explain the cultural roots of these, and an appreciation of the ways those norms and values are seen from other perspectives.
2. Students will demonstrate **awareness of other cultures**: an understanding of the cultural norms and values specific to their host culture, and an ability to value and explain the positive aspects of cultural differences.
3. Students will demonstrate **competencies for appropriate and effective interaction models:** an understanding of specific communication differences, a desire to respond in appropriate ways, and an ability to interact effectively.

These are just a few ideas about how you can develop learning goals for intercultural competence. You should structure your learning goals for students in ways that make sense to you.

Once you've defined the components of intercultural compentence, how can you actually teach or facilitate students' development of these in the study abroad context? As previously noted, we cannot expect that students will automatically gain this competence just by being abroad; they need direction and assistance. But unlike content taught in a traditional classroom, the development of this competence comes in part from the experience of being abroad, and in part from within the student. How do faculty both teach and not teach this? Is that even possible? In the next section, we'll look at learning and teaching theories to build a pedagogy that will facilitate this growth and learning.

CHAPTER 2

How Can We Help Students Learn? Building the Pedagogy to Achieve Learning Outcomes

"If we want to transform student learning,
we must transform our teaching." –L. Dee Fink

Learning and Teaching Models

Whether or not you've studied abroad yourself, or taken students abroad before, study abroad teaching and learning probably conjures up ideas of students' eyes and minds lighting up with new knowledge and experiences that deeply impact and transform them. Maybe this actually happened to you as a student—an amazing moment during a conversation or tour or site visit that led to a deep "aha" moment—or maybe you saw this in a student as you led him or her, figuratively and literally, through an experience.

This truly deep learning—transformational learning—marries two elements: experiences and knowledge-building. Experiences alone do not guarantee learning; without guidance and structure, students may walk right through experiences without constructing and articulating meaning. And even though we have a sense that meaning-making comes naturally to us as humans and that we are always trying to make sense of our experiences, one of the goals of intercultural development is to see our experiences in new ways. Without guidance and structure, our students' experiences will likely continue to be framed within the same worldviews and perspectives they started with. For this reason, the guidance of educators is crucial for transformational learning in education abroad.

Furthermore, as previously mentioned, simply being abroad does not guarantee students will even have experiences to make meaning from. If students are not nudged to move outside their comfort zones, to engage and interact and experiment, they may never even have those moments upon which to reflect. It is for this reason that many study abroad programs advocate for "intervention" or study abroad courses to help students develop intercultural competence. Like many, I have offered such a course, and in its initial stages I found that just asking students to write about their experiences wasn't enough. In spite of following the best practices for intervention—creating thoughtful prompts, setting aside space for reflection, and giving them a grade for their work—students still did not produce meaningful and insightful work, and initially I was not sure why. For example, in early manifestations of this course, my final assignment asked students to:

> Reflect on an emotional encounter, a miscommunication, or a frustration. Now that you are away from the moment, can you identify more clearly what led to the situation? What were you expecting to happen, and what actually happened? Is this a cultural norm that you misunderstood? What was your role in the misunderstanding?

The number of students who told me, after a full semester abroad, that they couldn't think of anything to write about was very troubling to me. I spent a lot of time thinking about how to help students have these valuable, transformative experiences, and more importantly to recognize them when they occur. Obviously, we cannot manufacture experiences, but it seems we can do more to place students in situations where valuable experiences are more likely to occur, and to provide students with the structure to stop and make sense of these experiences.

Initially I felt that in order to give students assignments that would lead to crucial, perspective-altering experiences, and in order to help guide them through the knowledge-making of these experiences, I needed to be an expert myself in each of their host cultures. While I felt somewhat qualified to do this for the countries where I had studied myself, I felt much less prepared for the many other countries where my students were studying. I swirled between trying to adapt secondary education curriculum guides on world studies, which felt too basic, and reflective writing assignments, which felt too vague and unstructured, continuously searching for assignments and rubrics upon which to base my course—all the while becoming increasingly frustrated.

I finally realized the place to start was with learning theory. Without understanding how students learn, and how study abroad experiences can best work, we cannot help them achieve transformational learning. And while there are hundreds of books about college teaching, second language acquisition, reflective learning, and flipped classrooms, there are not many resources on pedagogies for developing intercultural competence in education abroad. However, education abroad certainly draws upon these kinds of learning experiences—in addition to providing its own unique learning opportunities. After much research and firsthand experience teaching intercultural courses, I've developed the PRISM model to incorporate these approaches and apply them in an education abroad setting. This pedagogy blends opportunities for unstructured experiences that are the hallmarks of studying abroad with the structure needed for learning. In the PRISM model, educators provide ways for students to ***Get Prepared, Make it Relevant, Get Involved, Make Sense***, and ***Make it Matter***, all key elements in transformational learning.

Over the past eight years I have taught and honed this model in both online and face-to-face courses, and I have seen the positive results of other faculty using this model in faculty-led programs abroad. I have found the model lends itself to adaptation by length, location, purpose, and educator.

In the PRISM model I have incorporated elements from the pedagogical pillars of Kolb's Experiential Learning Theory, Bloom's Taxonomy, and Fink's Significant Learning Model, and translated them into approaches for educators in education abroad. On their own, each of these theories adds something to intercultural learning, but each also has some limitations. I have combined these models with my own knowledge and experience in education abroad to create PRISM: a rich, multifaceted learning approach.

As we tend to think of studying abroad first and foremost as experiential, let's look first at experiential learning. Kolb's Experiential Learning Theory (ELT) suggests that in order to learn from a **concrete experience** we need some intentional steps: first, time for **reflection,** next, construction of new knowledge, called **abstract conceptualization,** and then finally, testing of the knowledge in **active experimentation** . . . which leads to the next **concrete experience**. The result is a cycle: the student experiences, reflects, constructs, and acts.

Unfortunately, without guidance and support, this theory can break down in practice. For example, in the concrete experience phase, students

The Experiential Learning Cycle (Kolb 1984, 2015):

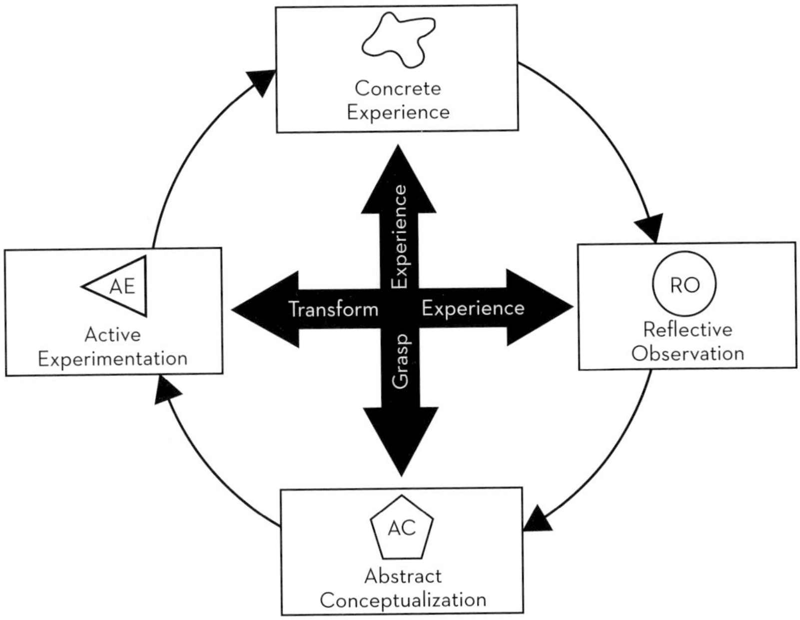

need to have an experience from which they can derive learning. In the study abroad context, we as educators may assume that these experiences occur organically and repeatedly, yet for many students and programs, this is not the case. If the program is structured so that students rarely meet and interact with locals in social and unscripted ways, the students have no chance for concrete experiences. Or, moving on to the reflective observation phase, if the program does not structure time for reflection, it is less likely that students will take time to reflect on their own, or, if they do, they may lack the tools and critical thinking or meta thinking to make meaning through their reflections. In the abstract conceptualization phase, students again need time, effort, and faculty guidance. Finally, in the active experimentation phase, students may struggle to have both the opportunity to interact and the courage to do so.

Study abroad programs are a prime opportunity to utilize ELT, but students need guidance to do so. "Educators have the opportunity to guide students from merely participating in activities to making meaning of their experiences" (Guthrie and Bertrand 2012, 59), but faculty may be unused to educating in this manner. ELT relies on faculty to facilitate rather than direct the learning process, so faculty need to be willing to accept a less teacher-centric role, allow students to experiment and discover solutions on their own, and share their own feelings and thoughts as they co-learn from the process themselves. For many faculty, this is a fairly significant shift in their sense of their role, from "conveyor of knowledge to facilitator of student learning" (Novak 2011, 72). Not only might ELT seem too unstructured to faculty, it may also seem unacademic. And even when faculty can recognize the learning occurring, it may seem difficult to measure, rate, or give feedback. The PRISM responds to this by providing a taxonomy of approaches and a rubric for measuring work products.

For something more familiar to faculty, Bloom's Taxonomy could be a guiding framework. Bloom's Taxonomy organizes six "cognitive processes," or categories of what educators want students to do with the information they acquire (Anderson and Krathwohl 2001). In this theory, the six cognitive processes build on one another, becoming increasingly complex, from simply remembering information to creating something new with the information. The six cognitive processes of Bloom's Taxonomy are **remember**, **understand**, **apply**, **analyze**, **evaluate**, and **create**.

The first cognitive process, **remember**, refers to the process of retrieving relevant knowledge from long-term memory, such as memorizing and citing facts, assigning items to categories, or recalling and reciting definitions. The subsequent five cognitive processes focus on increasingly complex ways in which students make sense of this knowledge and use what they have learned; in other words, engage in "knowledge construction" or "transfer of knowledge." **Understand** is the process of building connections between the new knowledge gained and their prior knowledge, such as providing examples of a phenomenon, summarizing, predicting outcomes, or providing rationales and justifications. **Apply** involves using procedures or applying facts and principles to perform exercises or solve problems. It may include practicing a new task or solving an unfamiliar problem. **Analyze** is deconstructing information into parts, determining how parts are related to each other, and reorganizing into a whole. Learning activities and assessments in this category ask students to find the relevance or relationship of different aspects of a problem or situation, describe the evidence supporting an outcome, or identify the function of a practice. Next is **evaluate,** the process of making judgments based on criteria or standards. Learning activities and assessments include explaining a value, justifying a position, or reframing an argument. Finally, **create** is the process of putting elements together into a new pattern or structure not clearly present before. Create involves the construction of a new product or idea.

Bloom's Taxonomy is likely familiar to faculty, and the idea of using this pedagogical framework for study abroad courses may feel like a workable approach in some regards. Bloom's Taxonomy shows us that there are similar cognitive processes in constructing knowledge from lectures and in making meaning from experiences. Educators may still struggle, however, in creating intercultural learning experiences and work products for students that utilize Bloom's Taxonomy. Intercultural development and intercultural learning outcomes are reliant upon students experiencing cultural elements, not necessarily upon the faculty providing lectures. This presents the dual challenge of releasing control from a typical lecture-style classroom and creating learning activities that promote the development of the desired competencies. The PRISM provides an answer to this by offering a semistructured approach for students to interact and experience the local culture, along with a structure for faculty to facilitate and respond to the learning.

A third model worth exploring is Fink's model for "Creating Significant Learning Experiences" (2013). Fink defines significant learning experiences as those which produce significant and lasting change for the student and provide meaningful value to them by enhancing their individual lives, preparing them to participate in multiple communities, or preparing them for the workforce.

Fink further asserts that significant learning experiences come when students are engaged in their learning within an active rather than passive learning environment. Research shows that passive learning environments, such as lecturing, have limited effectiveness in helping students retain information after a course is over, transfer knowledge to novel situations, develop motivation for additional learning, or change their attitudes (Fink 2013). However, lecturing often becomes the *modus operandi* for professors because students do not come prepared or do not participate, or simply because this has been the traditional way of teaching at a university.

Fink proposes an approach to learning that promotes active learning and thus results in more significant learning experiences. Rather than the cyclical approach of Experiential Learning Theory or the hierarchical approach of Bloom's Taxonomy, Fink proposes an interactive approach with six categories of learning which are relational, meaning students can work on them in any order or even simultaneously. The categories of learning include foundational knowledge, application, integration, human dimension, caring, and learning how to learn. **Foundational knowledge** is understanding and remembering specific information and ideas, providing a basic *understanding* necessary for other kinds of learning. **Application** involves learning how to engage in some new kind of action (intellectual, physical, or social), allowing the learning to be *useful.* **Integration** is being able to see and understand the connections between elements, giving learners a new form of *power*, especially intellectual power. **Human dimension** focuses on individuals learning something important about themselves or about others, enabling them to function and interact more effectively and recognize the *human significance* of what they are learning. **Caring** involves developing new feelings, interests, or values based on a learning experience, resulting in individuals dedicating the *energy* to learning more about it and making it part of their lives. **Learning how to learn** refers to learning how to be a better learner, how to engage in a particular kind of inquiry, or how to be a self-directed learner, enabling students to *continue* learning with *greater effectiveness.*

Fink's taxonomy helps teachers and students in that it includes not only content mastery but also relevance, connection, and meaning. This taxonomy's learning goals work in concert with one another—for example, students may increase content mastery because they see the relevance of it, or students may take the risk of application because they care about it. At this point you probably see the many ways this would be helpful in the classroom, although making it apply to the very different situation of education abroad may still seem elusive. The PRISM provides that application.

The PRISM incorporates these pedagogical theories and provides specific learning approaches to help students develop intercultural competence. The PRISM features five techniques or tools to help students learn from their experiences abroad. These techniques connect the cognitive process of Bloom's Taxonomy, while also helping students with the behavioral and attitudinal components of Experiential and Significant Learning theories. They engage students actively, while also giving them the language of intercultural learning to make sense of their experiences.

With the PRISM, I show you how to design learning activities, give you suggested assignments and rubrics, and help you bring together the best of pedagogical research. The PRISM model gives you *mechanisms* to facilitate learning while also giving students the *steps* to progress. The PRISM will help students Get **Prepared**, Make it **Relevant**, Get **Involved**, Make **Sense**, and Make it **Matter** in order to grow in their intercultural competence. The purpose and goal of each of these pedagogical techniques are as follows:

Tool	Purpose
Get PREPARED	Introduce the concept and generate thinking or conversation
Make it RELEVANT	Connect theory and content to experiences
Get INVOLVED	Encourage engagement with people
Make SENSE	Provide structure for students to think deeply and analyze
Make it MATTER	Provide opportunities to transfer knowledge

These five learning techniques, as I will define in the following pages, incorporate existing learning theories as well as provide something new for your teaching.

Get PREPARED

The first thing we want to help students do is ***get prepared*** – not just to travel, but to learn. We know from educational research that students learn best when they are invested in their own learning and take ownership of the learning experience. Similar to Fink's *learning how to learn* or Bloom's *remember* cognitive process, this tool is about helping students begin working on the knowledge and skills needed for effective and appropriate interaction *before* they even have cultural encounters.

Unfortunately, it can be a struggle to convince students to prepare before class or before travel. Even when students receive grade points for reading or coming prepared, many do not prepare, especially when they think that they will just pick up the needed knowledge and skills along the way.

In the PRISM methodology, I suggest using *prompts* or *primers* to *get students prepared.* This can take the form of icebreaker activities or thoughtful quotes and warm-up assignments to prepare students to engage. While in some ways this may seem simplistic, it is foundational, and particularly important given that students have different backgrounds of exposure to other cultures at the start of a study abroad experience.

Get prepared activities allow you to set the tone for learning and engage the students in different ways. For example, I could assign a reading and open the class with asking students what they thought about the reading, and then *tell them* how to apply the content from the reading to their time abroad . . . or, I could assign a reading, open the class with the icebreaker, and *ask them* how they applied the content from the reading. Using the icebreaker helps the students connect the theoretical to the real life in a more accessible way. One way I've done this is to bring in a fellow faculty member who was a former Peace Corps Volunteer in Papua New Guinea; she sits on the floor with students and for ten minutes speaks to them in Tok Pisin, describing pictures and artifacts and asking them questions. We then spend the rest of the class discussing their reactions to the experience: making connections to the reading, brainstorming strategies for success, and considering implications for their time abroad.

Get prepared activities can also serve as a type of *Just in Time Teaching* or *JiTT* (Mintz and Aagaard 2012: 488), where faculty help students apply learning just in time for problem-based activities, assignments, or classroom discussions. For example, I could help students *get prepared* by sharing advice such as "The most interesting things in life happen just on the other side of your comfort zone" (Michael Hyatt) to get students primed to think and act in ways that will facilitate their learning. Then, at the end of the day or week, I could ask them to think about ways they have practiced this approach (both at home and while abroad) and in what ways they want to keep this in the forefront of their minds as they move forward. With *get prepared*, the goal is to provide tools and mechanisms frequently and repeatedly, so students feel prepared to apply their learning when opportunities arise.

While it is hard to extrapolate the impact of *get prepared* activities, they do resonate with and motivate students. One student wrote the following to me about being inspired by the above quote on moving outside your comfort zone:

> Today I went to a local run club based out of the LuluLemon store in Leister Square. I love to be outside and active and while I absolutely love exploring the streets of London walking, it is difficult to find places to run and not irritate people. Plus, the park by my dorm does not seem to be in the nicest area. So, I decided to go out of my comfort zone and go by myself to run with a bunch of strangers. I have to admit that I was nervous. I do not mind being by myself at all, but it was still a nerve-racking situation, because I did not know what I was getting myself into. However, I am very proud of myself for putting myself out there and experiencing something new. The run was three miles long, and I met a bunch of new people of all ages, men and women. I also saw sights that I never would have seen. We ran along the Thames River, under the bridges, and over them. The lights were absolutely stunning at night, and it was something that I never could have done alone. Not only would I have gotten terribly lost, but I would not have been safe. I felt safe with the group. We ran through pouring rain, and it was a bonding experience. I was soaked and cold when I got back, but so excited. I thoroughly plan on going again next week and creating a routine out of it.

It is exciting to see students take advantage of opportunities to interact and engage while abroad, and while we may think that students who study abroad will just naturally seek out new experiences, helping them *get prepared* can prompt them to do this even more. In this case, we see her reiterate the language of "go out of my comfort zone" as the prompt to do something different which, in her opinion, led her to a positive, rewarding outcome.

With the PRISM, we are encouraging students to seek out new experiences and make meaning from them. *Get prepared* sets the stage for both of these, in motivating students to try new experiences and guiding students to make meaning from them.

Make it RELEVANT

Once we have prepared students for learning abroad, we want to provide readings and resources and ask students to make the material ***relevant*** to their experiences. In doing this, students can build a framework for understanding their experiences in deep and meaningful ways. Without such a framework, students will either not know how to interpret their experiences, or will do so from their original, often limited, perspectives. Having students connect relevant information, models, and paradigms to their personal experiences draws upon the cognitive process of *understand* from Bloom's Taxonomy, in which students build connections between their new knowledge and their prior knowledge (Anderson and Krathwohl 2001, 70). Fink calls this developing *foundational knowledge,* which provides a basic foundation necessary for interpreting and applying knowledge later on.

The key part of this process is not just providing a groundwork of relevant information but asking students to relate this to their experiences. In their principles of acquisition, Hattie and Yates state students are more likely to understand and learn if they are provided a model or construct for understanding. "We benefit enormously from being shown how to group information, how to locate patterns, how to use order, and how to schematize and summarize. Often we need to be taught a 'coat hanger' (or higher order concept) on which to hang new knowledge" (2013, 115).

In intercultural learning, the "coat hangers" or frames can be models for how culture and socialization work, models for seeing and understanding new perspectives, or models for recognizing privilege and power, for example. One model for how culture and socialization work is the concept of "cultural scripts," described in *Cultural Intelligence* as the patterns and ways of acting that we are socialized to use (Thomas and Inkson 2009). Below a student draws on this to begin building a framework for her experience:

> When I first told people I was going to Spain, many people commented how I would blend right in because I have darker skin, and dark brown hair. Because of this, I wasn't expecting to feel very different or like an outsider. However, I was very wrong. Even walking down the street I feel like an American and I feel like everyone can tell. I don't know if it is the way I dress, although I feel like I don't dress much differently than people here, or if it is something else. I even have the same type of hair as many girls here, but even so I feel like it is easy to tell that I am American. This has been an odd feeling for me because I am used to traveling to other places for a week or two [when I expected] to feel like a visitor or outsider. However, now that I have been living here for over a month, feel comfortable here, and know my way around, I feel like it is still very obvious that I am American. I believe in many ways I feel different because I operate on a different script, like it says on page 48—"we observe and make sense of others' actions based on [our own] scripts." While I operate based on my own script, everyone else here has their own script, and I have not quite yet figured out how those two work together. Maybe even the way I cross the street and carry my backpack are different—also the fact that I am usually walking around to and from school alone, when many Spaniards are always together.

Although she does not yet have the answers, she is able to frame the question in more sophisticated terms than simply, "I feel different," to "I feel different because I operate on a different script." This seemingly simple statement, and the ones that follow, show openness (she uses the word "different," not "wrong" or "weird"), cultural self-awareness (she identifies behaviors that may mark her as American), awareness of cultural frameworks (she recognizes there are "scripts" directing people's actions and interpretations), and curiosity (she states a desire to uncover how to adapt to their script or understand what it is that they interpret about her). She is beginning to recognize the aspects of culture that may impact her interactions and interpretations by making the concept in the reading *relevant* to her experiences.

The "coat hangers," frames, or models can come from readings, videos, TED talks, and/or lectures, and are essential for providing the grounding and context for students to move beyond observing to understanding. In the study abroad context, students may need both micro, culture-specific information, and macro, theoretical information. On a culture-specific level, it is helpful to connect visible behaviors and manifestations to underlying values and thought patterns that allow students to better understand the culture. For example, you may encourage your students in France to greet service workers with formal greetings and titles ("Bonjour, Madame"), but equally important is helping students appreciate how this is connected to an underlying value of respect for more formal, distant, and hierarchical social relationships. Helping students *make it relevant* in this context can include asking them to discover other ways this value manifests itself, and discussing reasons why this value makes sense and works in the settings it does. Culturally specific interactional advice can be found in sources such as CultureGrams™ (http://www.culturegrams.com/), cultural etiquette guides, travel books, and more.

On a macro, theoretical level, it is important to help students understand the ways cultures work as deeply ingrained social systems. There is no shortage of wonderful materials to help students understand the larger frameworks of how culture works or what empathy is. One of my favorite resources for a provocative and eye-opening look at frames of understanding is the TED Talk "A Radical Experiment in Empathy" by Sam Richards. In this engaging talk, Richards encourages listeners to recognize that how we perceive and interpret information is strongly determined by our history, orientation, culture, biases, and power. This TED talk evokes strong emotions but can also lead to incredible new insights. I ask students to watch this and then lead a discussion of what empathy really means, and how hard it is to understand others when it means recognizing that *they* think *we* are wrong.

To help students interpret their experiences, see new perspectives, and understand new ways of thinking, we must give them *resources* to do so, such as readings, TED talks, or class lectures. When it comes to education abroad in particular, students need resources because, while we may not necessarily test the students on their understanding in a traditional way, we are asking them to understand at the moment of the cultural encounter and beyond. So encouraging students to connect or make the resources *relevant* to their experiences not only helps in the moment but also builds their intercultural competence.

Get INVOLVED

At the core of the study abroad experience is, of course, engaging in the local site. ***Getting involved*** is how students do this. While this seems simple, there are a few stumbling blocks that keep students from getting involved in organic and seamless ways and therefore require the intentionality of the ***get involved*** tool. First, students may not seek out intercultural interactions or may have trouble finding opportunities to do so. With shorter and more group-structured programs, students are often more isolated from their host culture, and having intercultural encounters is not always as easy as it seems.

Second, students may need direction and framing to approach intercultural interactions with respectful curiosity. They may not know where to meet people or how to ask questions. We cannot assume students will have "a set of cognitive, affective, and behavioral tools for effective and appropriate interactions in other cultures" to begin with, and so they may need assistance to get involved.

Finally, *getting involved* as a mechanism for learning can be very unfamiliar and uncomfortable for students. It is estimated that by the time students are in college, they have spent ten thousand hours sitting and listening (standupkids.org) and only a fraction of that time being more active learners, yet there is a great deal of research on the benefits of more active learning. For Kolb, this kind of *concrete experience* is the basis for any experiential learning endeavor. Fink encourages active learning through *application*, or learning how to engage in some new kind of action (intellectual, physical, or social), which he claims makes the learning feel useful.

What makes this unique in study abroad contexts is that, while we may or may not be asking students to do "new" activities, we are nearly always asking students to do them with unfamiliar people and in perhaps unfamiliar ways. *Get involved* gives students both the opportunity and the structure by providing them with ideas, activities, questions, and assignments.

A *get involved* activity for study abroad students could be asking students to go to a different religious service or talk to a shopkeeper about his or her products. As before, they can be general or culture specific, but the role of the educator is to keep pushing the student to interact and engage with locals. Furthermore, it is important to remind students that to learn from locals, they need to approach people with genuine curiosity and respect. You can help them *get prepared* by reminding them that (to paraphrase the popular quote) "everyone is a genius, as long as you don't judge a fish by its ability to climb."

Get involved assignments can feel contrived and maybe even awkward or intimidating. Students may feel more comfortable if they have the freedom to adapt the assignment, so long as the intention of the assignment is still there. You and the students could even create assignments together; this gives them ownership and excitement. Students should look for all sorts of opportunities to *get involved*—with cab drivers, hotel workers, shop owners, etc. Students may feel more comfortable doing interaction assignments in groups. If they wish to take photos or record videos, students should always ask for permission beforehand and treat individuals with dignity.

In addition, we want students to engage in unstructured ways. *Get involved* assignments can incorporate this by either providing very generic instruction, such as "go to a market," or "take someone out to lunch," or by simply asking students to report back on interactions. The key is to hold students accountable for interacting with people in the host culture.

Below is one student's example of how she has been prompted to *get involved*:

> After reading the chapter on developing cultural intelligence, I realize now that I'm only somewhere around stage two or three in the development of my skills, despite how open-minded I believe that I am. I hope that the study abroad experience gets me one step closer to stage five. "The acquisition of cultural intelligence involves learning from social interactions" (Thomas and Inkson 156). How can you gain that knowledge without placing yourself in other cultures, and most importantly, interacting with them? I've noticed that it is often the same 2-3 people working in small shops and restaurants, so to practice my interaction skills, I have been going to the same places to develop somewhat of a relationship with the workers. I even get discounts in a few places! This is a perfect way for me to practice my Italian, and even ask them a few questions about their culture as I enjoy one of their paninis.

This student recognizes the value of interacting and developing relationships. Despite being a beginning language learner, recognizing the importance of *getting involved* has led her to language improvements, new cultural understandings, and a more local experience.

Make SENSE

For students to learn from their experiences, they need to spend some time ***making sense*** of them. Significant research shows we learn best when there are mechanisms for processing, checking, and experimenting with new meanings (Jordi 2011, Moon 2004, Wagner and Magistrale 2000, Kolb 1984), such as searching for patterns, interpreting (and reinterpreting) data, or drawing conclusions through conversation, writing, or practicing new skills. The "transformative effects" of experiential learning "depend on careful planning and execution, on avoiding the tendency to fall back on the adage that 'every experience is educational,' and on pushing students—and faculty—to think rigorously and extensively about the intersections between theory and practice" (Jordi 2011, 11). Fink calls this *integration*: being able to see and understand the connections. In the Bloom taxonomy, this is called *analyze.*

Often, this *making sense* falls under the rubric of "reflection," which has been cited as an important piece of the learning process (Moon 2004,

Wagner and Magistrale 2000, Kolb 1984). Reflection fosters critical thinking, encourages self-expression, improves communication and observational skills, and gives students a sense of ownership in their learning (Mair 2012, Kennison 2012, Moon 2004, Wagner and Magistrale 2000). Written reflection is particularly touted as a learning tool in study abroad. Writing, even before you fully understand or have all the pieces, forces you to structure, organize, and articulate your thoughts, in effect testing and teaching yourself at the same time (Carey 2014). But writing is not the only way to do reflection; reflective discussion can also be used, and can take place in a group as well as individually.

However, students often resist doing reflective work or struggle to do it well. Students "tend to care more about doing the work than about reflecting on it" (Moore 2010, 10). If the program does not provide some structure for reflection, it is not likely that students will do it on their own. Or, if they do, they may have difficulty doing quality and meaningful reflection; students tend to write more personal and emotional reflections rather than analytical and insightful reflections.

This is because students often need not only the time and space to reflect, but also *stimuli* and prompting. Stimuli and prompting give students a mechanism for framing and explaining their experiences rather than just relaying them. The PRISM pedagogy is important because it provides the structure that comes from dedicated time and space as well as provocative questions, such as "*How do you think your culture has shaped you? How has it influenced your values, preferences, and beliefs?*" to elicit thoughtful reactions. This provides opportunities for the students to *make sense* of their experiences and connect them to broader concepts.

For a comparison of unprompted versus prompted reflection, I'll share two essays. One semester I divided my students into two sections. In the first section, I did not provide prompts for the writing. Instead, students were told each week to "Write a thoughtful, reflective journal entry of 350 to 500 words, reflecting on your cultural experiences for the week." Here is an example of selections from one student's essay for the last week of the semester:

> I have not discussed my other travels in my reflections yet, but I think it is an important topic. So far, I have been to Copenhagen, three cities in Ireland, Florence, and I am going to Paris in two weeks. These trips have been amazing! It is surreal that I am able to take weekend trips to these incredible places. I have experienced things I never imagined I would. I climbed to the top of the Duomo in Florence, explored the castle in Limerick, and saw the famous mermaid statue in Copenhagen. These trips have taught me many things in my time abroad.
>
> First, I learned that I never want to stop traveling and I learned how exactly I like to travel. . . . My trips also helped me realize how I prefer to travel. I am not a person who likes to hit as many cities as possible in a short amount of time. I would much rather spend a longer amount of time in the same city. I do not like being rushed if I am trying to enjoy a new city. Therefore, I like spreading out an itinerary over a few days so I can spend as much time as I want, wherever I want. I also think you get a better idea of the culture when you have the time to slow down. For example, I was in Copenhagen for three days and I got to discover parts of the city that were not just the major tourist attractions and those were my favorite parts of the city! . . .
>
> Another important thing I learned from my trips is that I am absolutely in love with London. Don't get me wrong, the places I am traveling to are incredible, but I am always looking forward to getting back to London. When I get back from my trips, I am overwhelmed with a sense of being home. It is an amazing feeling, knowing I picked the city that was a perfect fit for me.

This essay portrays a very individualistic approach of consuming the site, and even the reference to preferring to "spend a longer amount of time in the same city" still means only "spreading out an itinerary over a few days." She does not spend any time *making sense* of the sites she sees or even why London feels like home.

In the second section of this course, I gave students a prompt to help them *make sense* and also asked them to make the readings *relevant* to their experiences by incorporating something from the reading. The following essay was also submitted the last week of the semester, responding to the prompt, "Daydream about the future. How do you see yourself implementing the knowledge, skills, and perspectives you've gained as a part of this experience? What do you want to do next with your life? How will this experience help you in the future?" Interestingly, this student also writes about the experience of traveling throughout Europe, but she frames her writing by contrasting the experience of visiting versus staying and understanding.

> Upon studying abroad, I realize that traveling can only do so much. After hearing people coming back from weekends away, and looking back on trips myself, I realize that I may be seeing many things, but I am experiencing little.
>
> . . . How many times have I been to places and only seen, never experienced? The thought frightens me. I have learned how "the ability to deal effectively with others who are culturally different has become a daily necessity" (174). But I have also learned that I don't want to just 'deal' with these people, I want to become a part of these people. I want to integrate myself and become a part of this culture.
>
> Studying abroad has taught me the importance of listening, observing, and the importance of not just visiting but staying. A taste of London may not have brought me back. But this 7 course meal has left me satisfied, and excited to return. This place has won my heart, and shown me a multitude of cultures. The satisfaction you get when you know about other cultures, and the importance of always having an open mind and heart towards what you don't know. Studying abroad has made me who I am.

While both essays focus on travel, the first one emphasizes the sites visited without trying to make any sense of them or put them into any context. By contrast, the second essay analyzes and critiques the notion of visiting, stating that perhaps the goal instead should be seeing "what the locals do." The essay even challenges a passage from the reading, defining a more empathetic approach: rather than "to just 'deal' with people, I want to become a part of these people." The author indicates she has gained the skills of "having an open mind and heart towards what you don't know."

The *make sense* step provides an organizational framework for reflection and dedicated time to make meaning. Activities can include writing or discussing, and can take place in a group or individually, but the key is the faculty or educator needs to provide the time, space, and *facilitation* for students to reflect, and in particular the structure of prompt questions or guided conversations. Providing students the structure and framework for *making sense*—be it through prompted writing or guided conversation—can help students move from just traveling through other countries to having transformative learning experiences.

Make it MATTER

The final tool in PRISM is ***make it matter***. With this, we want to provide ways for students to think about the transfer of their knowledge and experiences to other scenarios. The goal of intercultural competence is not that students become experts in all cultures (which would be impossible anyway), but that they develop skillsets and adopt mindsets to interact in diverse settings. We want them to value and respect cultural differences and seek out differences to learn more. We want them to think critically about ways to continue engaging with people and issues in the world.

The goal with *make it matter* is to encourage students to articulate for themselves how they can apply their learning. This should move beyond the typical comments about wanting to travel the world or wanting to make all students study abroad; rather, in *make it matter* students should be able to address the deeper impact of their actions as related to intercultural development.

Make it matter is in some ways similar to the highest level cognitive processes in Bloom's Taxonomy, *evaluate* and *create*, and to Kohls's *abstract conceptualization*, but the manifestation of it is somewhat less structured. Sometimes *make it matter* is demonstrated in the student seeking out more cultural experiences. It may be demonstrated in the ways students approach interactions with more respect and empathy. Or it may be demonstrated in how the student educates others about cultural diversity and intercultural issues.

Up to this point, many of the PRISM approaches have been structured and immediate, but this is the opportunity for creative thinking and long-term impact. In the context of a study abroad term, a *make it matter* piece may be difficult to do, but there are certainly some approaches that will facilitate long-term impacts. One is to help students identify how to transfer the learning from the abroad context to future contexts. For example, you can ask students what they have learned, and what they want to do with what they learned. Ask them to think about the quotations and advice they were given in *get prepared*, or even to come up with their own new mantra. How will this guide them in the future? How will they be agents of change or activists with the competence they have gained? Or, you could use an essay or discussion prompt such as the following:

> What do you think it means to be a global citizen? What rights and responsibilities do you have if you are a global citizen? How are you better prepared to be a global citizen because of studying abroad?

The following response comes from an essay submitted by a student who spent a semester in London.

> Being a global citizen means having the right to explore other cultures but comes with the responsibility of exploring these other cultures without adding pre-existing stereotypes to the experience. Being a global citizen means having the right to interact with people from all around the world but comes with the responsibility of treating the people you meet with respect even when they do not share your opinion. Finally, being a global citizen means having the right to identify yourself with a chosen culture but comes with the responsibility to realize that though we may all be of different cultures, we are all human.

In this essay, the student beautifully and eloquently articulates the essence of intercultural competence: an understanding of cultural frameworks, empathy, curiosity, and openness. A first-generation college student, she had never traveled abroad prior to her study abroad semester. Although she stated in her application essay that her goal was to "find for myself what London has to offer so that I may fully appreciate the global community as a whole," her understanding of London before departure consisted of knowing that "people in London drive on the left side of the road, the currency used there is the pound sterling, and the government there is a monarchy." The level of understanding articulated in the short paragraph above shows remarkable growth from before departure to the end of her stay.

But even students with a great deal of international experience can benefit from the PRISM approach and from *make it matter* in particular. The following essay was submitted by a student at the end of her semester in Nice, France, in response to the same prompt.

> Before actually going to study abroad we were given the title of being "global scholars." However, I think I didn't actually know what it meant until I actually experienced it. I found out that being a global citizen is not just something that you are; it is a way of living. Being a global citizen is a lifestyle in which you are aware of choices and actions, and how they can make an impact locally or globally. Being a global citizen includes so many things like: having a sense of yourself and others, being responsible and able to make decisions and solve problems, and most importantly being culturally intelligent.
>
> As a global citizen we have rights and responsibilities. I believe the main right can be equity. Global citizens view every culture as being important and significant. They tolerate differences and treat everyone equal. There are many more responsibilities as well. First, being conscious of our actions and how they impact the world and others, being aware of global issues and making others aware of it too, being empathic and sensitive of these issues and differences. Our main responsibility is to make others aware of world different cultures, issues and their actions so that they can become global citizens too. All of these efforts join to make us better people and create a better world.
>
> Studying abroad really helps to become a better global citizen because it puts in daily practice the factors I mentioned. You face differences between cultures every day, even different language. Now I can talk with people of different cultures without feeling a barrier between us, because I understand better their feelings. I am able to change my behavior because of different cultural situations, I can clearly say how we are different but I accept it. I am able to see how their culture influences the world and me and how my culture influences them as well.

Interestingly, while she is originally from Ecuador and had spent two years in the US before studying in Nice, she attributes her transformation into a global citizen to her time in Nice. Presumably she had already been applying these characteristics during her time in the US as an international student. However, throughout her time in my course, and in particular in this final essay while abroad, she more thoroughly explores the concepts of intercultural learning and specifically articulates how her time in Nice has given her a chance to practice these skills. No doubt both of her experiences of living abroad have contributed to her skillset and attitudes, but the *make it matter* assignment provided, for this student and for many others, a place for synthesizing learning, a structure for deciding on actions, and an incentive to launch their learning forward.

You can also ask students to begin to think about how they will share their experience and contribute to the education of others. What stereotypes do they hope to dispel when they return? Or, if you have the ability to interact with them after they return, you can have them start discussing their experiences, such as:

> Describe a time you felt someone here misunderstood something about your host culture or your experience abroad. Did you correct their perception? What else could you have said?

One student who spent a semester in Belgium shared the following with me:

> Coming back to school in the US is difficult for anyone who studies abroad because you have transformed in many ways, but your friends and family at home often expect you to be the same. As much as I wanted to share my experience in my host country, most of my friends simply didn't want to hear about it. Their interest was focused on their preconceived ideas of study abroad—an international vacation full of crazy drinking and partying. Nearly everyone I spoke to assumed that my classes were easy As, which they certainly were not. I attempted to explain the strict structure of my classes, the difficult adjustments for studying habits, and the invaluable lessons I had learned from a variety of professors and peers. . . . My friends also assumed that the extent of my cultural exposure was trying new beers and taking pictures with famous monuments. While there was plenty of that, I wish I would have told them about the everyday experiences that made all the difference. Everything from figuring out which bus to take,

> to my need to find a trash bag getting lost in translation with the French shopkeeper, to struggling to find a new friend to eat lunch with, made life a little more complicated. It was often the mundane experiences that gave me a new perspective of my American lifestyle. How could I explain this to someone who hadn't seen it themselves? I truly believe that the most effective learning is through experience and that the only way to overcome these misconceptions is to encourage students to study abroad themselves.

The student describes her efforts to reframe the conversations she had to give a more complete and nuanced picture of her experience and of Belgians. While she feels frustrated that she was not successful, she articulates a high level of flexibility through describing the "difficult adjustment for studying habits" and "struggling" with transportation and language and friendships. She also articulates a sense of advocacy to "encourage students to study abroad themselves" in order to better understand the misconceptions. Again we see how *make it matter* provides a platform for students to articulate what mattered from their experiences and how they want to move forward with their newfound knowledge and skills.

A final way you can use *make it matter* is to encourage students to apply their learning in new and creative ways, such as getting involved with international students at their school or the international community in their city, or getting involved in international issues through advocacy or fundraising. You may be able to incentivize this through assignments, awards, or funds, or by simply presenting opportunities for them to act. For example, at TCU we have been gifted with an award for study abroad students, and we have decided to present it annually to an undergraduate study abroad student who exhibits global citizenship following their time abroad by engaging in a significant project or activity that exemplifies internationalization. Award winners' projects have included establishing the Rwanda Student Organization and implementing TCU's 20th Commemoration of the Rwanda Genocide, organizing a book drive for the children at the Missahoe Children's Home in Kpando, Ghana, and spearheading a team that raised more than $20,000 for local and international organizations fighting human trafficking.

The goal with *make it matter* is to encourage the students to articulate for themselves what they want to do with their learning and how they might make that happen. Encourage them to think in terms of both small and big actions; they needn't all aspire to become the Secretary of State or the next ground-breaking activist to make a difference. We all have an impact in our families, communities, schools, neighborhoods, and voting districts, to broaden viewpoints, promote cross-cultural problem-solving, and engage proactively both locally and globally.

Conclusion

The five techniques of the PRISM—***Get Prepared, Make it Relevant, Get Involved, Make Sense***, and ***Make it Matter***—provide a multifaceted framework for guiding students through their cultural experiences to help them develop intercultural competence. These techniques combine pedagogical best practices with site-based learning, resulting in student development on cognitive, behavioral, and affective levels. In using the PRISM, educators can employ a variety of approaches, and students can engage with the material in a variety of ways, resulting in truly transformational experiences. In summary, the PRISM techniques work as follows:

Tool	Purpose	Educator Provides
Get PREPARED	Introduce the concept and generate thinking or conversation	Quotes for conversation Icebreaker activities Warm-up activities
Make it RELEVANT	Connect theory and content to experiences	Readings Videos Lectures
Get INVOLVED	Encourage engagement with people	Structured activities Unstructured activities
Make SENSE	Provide structure for students to think deeply and analyze	Writing prompts Guided discussion
Make it MATTER	Provide opportunities to transfer knowledge	Follow-up activities Quotes for conversation

As you move forward in applying the PRISM to your study abroad program or class, keep not only the tools themselves but the broader metaphor in mind. How can students have richer experiences? How can they see these experiences in more multifaceted ways? How can they act in more thoughtful and nuanced ways? In the following chapter and appendices, I will provide you some concrete examples of activities, readings, assignments, and prompts for you to create your PRISM.

CHAPTER 3

How Do I Apply the PRISM? Building a Cache of Materials and Strategies for Developing Student Learning

"A goal without a plan is just a wish."
—Antoine de Saint-Exupéry

How Do I Apply the Prism?

In this chapter I will provide suggestions on how to use the PRISM for the development of intercultural competence. This includes both fleshing out intercultural competence as a ***goal*** and exploring how to apply the PRISM as the ***plan*** for achieving it.

As discussed in Chapter 1, intercultural competence is quite dense and unwieldy as a single concept, so I presented seven separate, albeit interrelated, components—cultural self-knowledge, ethnorelative understanding of cultural worldviews, culture-specific knowledge, empathy and respect, sociolinguistic awareness and intercultural communication skills, curiosity and discovery, and openness and flexibility—and suggested some ways to build a framework using these seven components. One suggestion was to make each of these components a discrete learning outcome, such as:

1. Students will articulate insights into their own cultural rules and biases (**Cultural Self-Knowledge**).
2. Students will identify the cultural elements that underlie and shape the viewpoints of others and respect them without judgment (**Ethnorelative Understanding of Cultural Worldviews).**
3. Students will articulate specific values, habits, norms, and their significance, typical of members of another culture (**Culture-Specific Knowledge**).
4. Students will demonstrate an ability to interpret intercultural experience from more than one worldview and an ability to act in a supportive manner that recognizes the feelings of culturally different others (**Empathy and Respect**).
5. Students will articulate an understanding of cultural differences in verbal and nonverbal communication and be able to skillfully negotiate a shared understanding based on those differences (**Sociolinguistic Awareness and Intercultural Communication Skills**).
6. Students will demonstrate an ability to ask complex questions

about other cultures and seek out answers to these questions that reflect multiple cultural perspectives (**Curiosity and Discovery**).

7. Students will demonstrate an ability to seek out interactions with different people and practice new, culturally appropriate behaviors (**Openness and Flexibility**).

But there are other ways to organize these elements. Given that these concepts are interrelated, I also suggested combining them in different ways to build your own learning outcomes, such as:

1. Students will demonstrate **cultural self-awareness**: an understanding of specific cultural norms and values, an appreciation of the ways those norms and values are seen from other perspectives, and an ability to explain cultural roots.
2. Students will demonstrate **awareness of other cultures**: an understanding of specific cultural norms and values and an ability to value and explain the positive aspects of cultural differences.
3. Students will demonstrate **competencies for appropriate and effective interaction models:** an understanding of specific communication differences, a desire to respond in appropriate ways, and an ability to interact effectively.

Once you determine your learning outcomes, you can use the PRISM as tools or student action steps to help students achieve these learning outcomes, so that it might look something like this:

Learning Outcome: Students will articulate insights into their own cultural rules and biases.

Student Action Steps:

1. Students will participate in class discussion based on **Get Prepared** quote, exploring their own cultural rules and biases.
2. Students will **Make it Relevant** by connecting readings and resources to their own experiences to describe their cultural rules and biases.
3. Students will **Get Involved** in conversations to explore their own cultural rules and biases.
4. Students will **Make Sense** of their own cultural rules and biases through class discussion and writing.

5. Students will **Make it Matter** by discussing how to incorporate new knowledge and understanding in their daily lives.

You could use all five PRISM tools for each learning outcome, or any of the tools that make the most sense to you. You can use some of the PRISM tools prior to departure, some while abroad, and some post return. The PRISM model allows you to design the implementation according to what works best for your program.

The table below is a reminder of the purpose of each learning tool of PRISM. In Chapter 2, I explained the learning theory behind these tools, and here I will show you how to use them in cultural learning settings by providing specific materials for each tool and strategies you can use for employing each tool. Some of these approaches may feel familiar to you even if the content or setting is new, or it all may feel very new to you, but either way it is useful to look at this in more depth to see how the learning tools of PRISM can be used to develop the learning outcomes of intercultural competence.

Tool	Purpose	Educator provides	Types of formats Educators can use
Get PREPARED	Introduce the concept and generate thinking or conversation	Quotes for conversation Icebreaker activities Warm-up activities	Email Post on website Discuss / do at start of class or orientation
Make it RELEVANT	Connect theory and content to experiences	Readings Videos Lectures	Assignments for class Posts on social media
Get INVOLVED	Encourage engagement with people	Structured activities Unstructured activities	Assignments for class Prizes or prestige for completion
Make SENSE	Provide structure for students to think deeply and analyze	Writing prompts Guided discussion	Assignments for class Prizes or prestige for completion
Make it MATTER	Provide opportunities to transfer knowledge	Quotes for conversation Give-back activities	Discussions at end of class Incorporation into post-return activities

To model how you can use the PRISM in your classroom or program, I will provide some specific examples of materials to use and methods to employ in classroom and programmatic ways.

Materials

As you begin to think about which materials you want to use, there are a couple of approaches. If you would like to use a single book for your activities and readings, below are some ideas. I have listed a brief overview of the strengths of each of these books, and in the next section I show more specifically how to connect them to the intercultural learning components. For those who would like to build in variety or solely use online materials, I suggest book chapters, TED talks, and other materials under each relevant intercultural learning component.

The following are books and resources that work well for **Get PREPARED** activities:

Berardo, Kate. and Darla K. Deardorff. *Building cultural competence: Innovative activities and models*. Sterling, VA: Stylus, 2012.

A creative and innovative set of training tools, models, and activities to use in diverse settings, framed around skillsets and knowledge sets essential for cultural competence.

Global Scholar. *http://GlobalScholar.us*.

A free, online set of courses with short student videos, activities, quizzes, and practical advice.

Kohls, L. Robert. and Knight, John. M. *Developing Intercultural Awareness: A cross-cultural training handbook*. Yarmouth, ME: Intercultural Press, 1994.

A wide range of icebreaker activities, with detailed instructions on materials needed, amount of time to run the activity, how to conduct the activity, and how to debrief afterwards.

Mompoint-Gaillard, Pascale. and Lazar, Ildaka. *TASKs for democracy: 60 activities to learn and assess transversal attitudes, skills, and knowledge,* 2015. Strasbourg: Council of Europe. Available at http://www.coe.int/t/dg4/education/pestalozzi/Source/Documentation/Pestalozzi4_EN.pdf

Creative activities in a variety of lengths with detailed instructions for organizing, implementing, and debriefing.

Stringer, Donna M. and Patricia A. Cassiday. *52 Activities for Improving Cross-Cultural Communication.* Yarmouth, ME: Intercultural Press, 2009.

Activity-based exercises; while particularly focused on intercultural communication skills, the activities here can also help foster knowledge of other cultures, openness, and empathy.

Below are some books and resources that can serve as your textbook or reader for students to **Make it RELEVANT** and/or can inform your teaching:

Hess, J. Daniel. *The Whole World Guide to Cultural Learning.* Yarmouth, ME: Intercultural Press, 1994.

An in-depth book including explanations of the cross-cultural adaptation process and methods for becoming an effective sojourner abroad.

Kohls, L. Robert. *Survival Kit for Overseas Living.* Yarmouth, ME: Intercultural Press, 2001.

Short and easily readable book covering tips for intercultural learning from a pragmatic point of view.

Paige, R. Michael, Andrew D. Cohen, Barbara Kappler, Julie C. Chi, James P. Lassegard. *Maximizing Study Abroad.* Minneapolis, MN: Center for Advanced Research on Language Acquisition, 2004.

An easy-to-read guide aimed at helping students identify and use a wide variety of language- and culture-learning strategies. The book uses self-assessment inventories to help students be more aware of how they learn language and culture and how they can use those strategies to make the most of their experiences.

Peterson, Brooks. *Cultural Intelligence.* Yarmouth, ME: Intercultural Press, 2004.

A short book geared toward professionals working abroad but still effective as a textbook, using case studies and illustrations to provide tips for working effectively with international clients, customers, and business partners.

Thomas, David and Inkson, Kerr. *Cultural Intelligence: Living and Working Globally.* San Francisco, CA: Berrett-Koehler Press, 2009.

An accessible text covering core concepts related to intercultural competence as well as anecdotal vignettes. Presents a goal of helping readers gain perspective and awareness and increase their CIQ (Cultural IQ).

Adichie, Chimamanda Ngozi. "The Danger of a Single Story." *TED Global.* http://www.ted.com/talks/chimamanda_adichie_the_danger_of_a_single_story.

An insightful TED talk from the Nigerian author exploring her own biases and those of people she's encountered and encouraging listeners to see people in more complex and multidimensional ways.

Riccardi, Pellegrino. "Cross Cultural Communication." *TEDxBergen.* https://www.youtube.com/watch?v=YMyofREc5Jk.

A funny, insightful TED talk covering perspective, values, curiosity, and communication across cultures.

Steves, Rick. "The Value of Travel." *TEDxRainier.* https://www.youtube.com/watch?v=kYXiegTXsEs.

An inspiring TED talk challenging tourists to become travelers and showcasing the ways we can better understand and appreciate the places and the people we visit.

For a great, use-anytime **Get INVOLVED** prompt, ask students to do the following:

Go to the market or to a shop and speak with a vendor. How long have they been selling the product? How did they become interested in selling the product? How did they gain expertise in the product? What would they like tourists or non-natives to know about the product?

This conversation can lead to insights about nearly every aspect of intercultural competence: host culture values, communication differences, curiosity, empathy, and openness.

To help students **Make SENSE** of their experiences, the following prompts are open enough to draw out all kinds of insights:

Look back at something you wrote about your host culture when you first arrived. Has your interpretation of this changed? Do you have more insight into the aspects you found strange, quaint, or confusing?

Describe a time you (pleasantly) surprised yourself while abroad. What did you do, and why did you do it? Why was this out of the ordinary for you?

Share a proverb, motto, or saying from your host culture. How and when do they use it? What insight does it give you?

Describe a food and/or mealtime experience. What is the meaning and significance of the food, its preparation, and/or the experience of eating it? What insight does this give you?

Describe a time you made a genuine cross-cultural connection. What was it, how, when, and why did it happen?

To help students **Make it MATTER,** the following prompt provides for great conversation and action:

What stereotypes—yours and theirs—do you find being challenged? How do you want to respond to stereotypes you encounter in the future?

Methods

Now, using these materials, I will show you how to apply the PRISM approach in a classroom or program setting. First, I will demonstrate in depth how to use each of the PRISM steps, using the learning outcome *students will articulate insights into their own cultural rules and biases.* Next, I will provide a PRISM lesson plan for the seven components of intercultural competence described in Chapter 1, offering example materials, action steps, and approaches.

Get PREPARED

Get Prepared is about engaging students in the learning process early on and setting the tone. I describe two approaches here: Quotes for Conversation and Warm-up Activities.

A *get prepared* action step might look like this:

Students will participate in class discussion based on *get prepared* quote, exploring their own cultural rules and biases.

Quotes for Conversation are quotes to give students prior to class or at the start of class not only to generate conversation but to encourage students to begin to take ownership of their own learning.

> *Example: Prior to class, provide this Quote for Conversation:*
>
> "It is not my place to doubt the sincere beliefs of others. My job is to question my own beliefs."
>
> —Jonathan Lockwood Huie

To generate conversation, after you provide the quote, you may say, "What do you think this means? How do you think you'll try to do this while abroad?" While some students may be eager to talk or may immediately understand the end goal, many will need help to move through even a short preparatory exercise. Here are some tips to help guide the conversation:

To draw students into a discussion, you may need to take baby steps. Using this quote as an example, let's break it down:

First, to even identify "my own beliefs," it might be helpful to think in contrast to what others believe. Ask students to identify some potential contrasts in beliefs between themselves and others. Don't be surprised if their answers are quite extreme or negative toward others. Remember, this is a starting point.

Students often respond well to tying in pop culture or current events. Ask them to think about the latest celebrity. What kinds of beliefs do they think this person has? Do they value these beliefs or not? Or ask them to think about times when they have had differences of opinion with other people—family members, friends, or bosses. Can they trace how an opinion might reflect a belief? Does this help them come closer to naming their own beliefs?

Next, ask them what they think it means to "not doubt the sincere beliefs of others." Does that mean to adopt them? Tolerate them? Referring to the already stated differences in beliefs of others, can they begin to think about how they might do better at not "doubting" them?

Then, ask them what it means to "question their own beliefs." What does that look like? Does it mean abandon them? Explore them? Ask them to think about what beliefs might be most difficult to question. What things are so fundamental to them that they cannot imagine they are not universally held? Examples might include:

> "I learned the value of hard work by working hard."
>
> —Margaret Mead (reflects a typical American value of work-orientation and sense of justice that work leads to success).
>
> "Believe you can and you're half-way there."
>
> —Teddy Roosevelt (reflects typical American value of optimism).

Can they imagine anyone not identifying with the above typical American beliefs? In a nonjudgmental way, can they imagine how these might not be values that others hold?

The end goal of this conversation is for students to begin to identify what beliefs are—both what their specific beliefs are and what belief is in the abstract sense—and to begin to recognize they hold some ideas they thought were universal standards but are actually beliefs.

Another type of *get prepared* exercise is Warm-up Activities, which simulate an experience you want to expose students to or provide an interactive way to demonstrate a concept.

One of my favorite activities from Kohls's and Knight's book is called *The Form*. I bring copies of it to class and ask students to complete it. They generally answer the first couple of questions before they start to really struggle, because the form asks questions that don't make sense to them and the lettering is written in mirror image. After the exercise, we talk about what was difficult to do and what strategies they used or could have used, such as asking questions, trying to problem-solve themselves (for example, flipping the paper over and holding up to the light makes the letters appear in a format they are used to), or any other strategies they came up with.

Icebreaker—The Form

- Goal: To understand the effects of cultural conditioning on people's ability to do a task.
- Group size: Variable.
- Materials: One copy of The Form for each participant and a few 3 x 5 white index cards with green magic marker lines drawn on them. There should also be a flip chart or board available for the discussion period.

Procedures

This exercise has a dual purpose. Initially, it can be used as a different kind of icebreaker to shock the participants into an awareness of how different cultures are and how visceral our reactions to these differences can be.

1. Distribute copies of The Form and the green-and-white cards. Each participant should receive a copy of The Form; the green-and-white cards should only be given to a select few. Then, read the following inflexible rules.
    - Write from right to left.
    - Write very clearly. Sloppy writing will be discarded.
    - Fill in every blank.
    - For #2 use the Moslem calendar, which begins July 16,

A.C. 622.

- Do not answer #7 unless you have a green-and-white card.
- Complete this task within three minutes.
- Ask no questions!

2. The initial discussion should focus on the participants' personal and cultural reactions to the exercise. Ask the participants how they felt during the exercise and record their responses, using single words or short phrases, on a flip chart or blackboard. Why did some use descriptions like "backwards," "stupid," or "frustrating," rather than "right to left" or "opposite from the way I usually write" to describe how they felt?

Additional questions can include:

- What does the word "blank" mean in the instructions, since there are both blank lines and blank spaces?
- Did the information about the Moslem calendar cause any problems?
- Was any of the information on the form confusing?
- Did the questions make sense? Why do you think they were asked? If you wanted to get to know someone, what questions would you ask?
- How many people actually finished the form?
- How did people cope with completing the form? In other words, who held the paper up to the light backward to read it, who wrote from left to right, and who just gave up?

Remember to keep the discussion open and free-flowing.

3. Close the exercise by discussing how we are culturally conditioned to view situations in predetermined ways and to respond to tasks in ways appropriate to our culture, as well as how we obtain information and how confused we are by other ways of doing so.

THE FORM

1. NAME ____________________
FAMILY??
BIRTH

2. YEARS

3. SEX YES ____________
NO ____________

4. STATUS
____

5. DEGREES
CHECK ONE O, V, X
PHD
PDQ
MA
AM
PM

6. FAVORITE COLOR
____
WHY? ____________________

7. LANGUAGE
YES ______ NO ______

8. IF ENGLISH
WHAT KIND
KOLAK
REGAN
EDITH

9. FAVORITE DISEASE

These example *get prepared* activities show you how to help students start thinking about cultural learning experiences and introduce the components they will need to develop intercultural competence.

Make it RELEVANT

Make it Relevant prompts students to connect the readings or resources to their experiences, so they can develop frameworks and models. Assigning materials to read or watch is a staple of academia, as a way to provide concepts for students to learn. The added piece here is helping students begin to relate their experiences to the concepts introduced, and at the same time elevate study abroad beyond simplistic stereotypes of sightseeing to transformational learning of intercultural concepts.

A *make it relevant* action step looks like this:

Students will *make it relevant* by connecting readings and resources to their own experiences to describe their cultural rules and biases.

Example: Assign students What is American Culture? at https://www.youtube.com/watch?v=4m-6mrGr4bY and "8 Cultural Differences between Native Speakers and English Learners" at https://www.youtube.com/watch?v=Tzx8ZJrFltU. (Despite the fact that he frames this as solely West versus East, the values he lists and the resulting behaviors are well explained and provide a great deal of insight into culture.) Discuss with students what they found insightful and relevant to themselves.

Many of the *make it relevant* resources provided here are online videos and TED talks, because I find that students really enjoy them, but in the same way that they have been taught how to retain information from reading (such as highlighting important points, making notes in the margins), they may need to be taught how to retain information from watching videos. I ask students to make notes as they are watching, recording such things as important points or thoughts they have while watching it. To further *make it relevant,* I ask students to come with at least one comment, question, or reaction they want to share with me and/or the class, and we use that to generate class discussion.

Get INVOLVED

Get Involved helps students engage in conversations with members of their host culture about topics they might not otherwise think to ask or in more in-depth ways than they might do without prompting.

A *Get Involved* action step might look like this:

Students will *Get Involved* in conversations to explore their own cultural rules and biases.

Example: Instruct students to ask a few locals how they perceive Americans. What assumptions do they have about American people?

For many, striking up conversations with people in other cultures can feel awkward, particularly if you are asking them to comment on values, norms, or habits. The goal of these conversations is not to delve into criticisms but rather to uncover insights. One students wrote:

> *Asking what some would consider a controversial question to a person of another country was a bit petrifying to me at first. Further into the semester, though, it became one of the greatest things I looked forward to each week.*

Encourage students first of all to begin to develop relationships with people by going to the same coffee shop or restaurant, or to pay attention to hotel staff (if that is where they are staying) and begin conversations with them, or to think about other people with whom they regularly interact (such as local program staff).

Then, to prepare for their assignments, ask students to think about framing their questions in a mutually beneficial way. In other words, not to approach people as purely "informants" but as experts who have something to teach. For example, the student may talk to someone at the hotel by first asking them, "Do you have a lot of Americans staying here? What are they typically here for? How long do they typically stay?" In doing this, they have given the other person a certain ethos or respect as an expert whose opinion is valued. The student can then move on to asking questions about how that person perceives Americans.

Students can also draw on their own experiences. For example, they might observe that there is always American music playing, and use that as a point of entry, as in "Wow, I didn't expect there to be so much American music here. Are there lots of American shows and movies too? In what other ways does the US influence everyday life here? What are your opinions of Americans?"

The goal is two-fold: first, for students to interact with local people in more equitable ways. Many times when we travel our interactions are hierarchical or transactional, with travelers expecting services and goods in exchange for money. With *Get Involved*, we are trying to shift the interactions to be more conversational. The second goal is for students to begin learning about different perspectives and views. The assignment questions are meant to be guides or prompts for students to seek out new knowledge. Students should be allowed to modify them in ways that make the conversation feel more natural, while still trying to uncover new insights about the overall topic.

Make SENSE

Processing and reflecting on experiences are essential parts of experiential learning, particularly as we try to push students to think in new ways or interpret with new worldviews. To help students ***Make Sense*** of their experiences through class discussion and writing, I encourage the use of prompts to help stimulate their thinking and organize their thoughts.

A *make sense* action step might look like this:

Students will *make sense* of their own cultural rules and biases through class discussion and writing.

> *Example: Instruct students: Think about your conversations, readings/TED talk, and class discussions, and respond to the following:*
>
> *Has anyone said something about the US that you found particularly insightful? What about it was insightful? How did it change your thinking about yourself and the US?*

Students often struggle with moving beyond simple reporting to interpreting. The key here is to remind them that they are trying to "make sense" of experiences. Hopefully when students do a *make sense* exercise they begin to bring in some of the learning from previous action steps as well as any informal learning. The prompts are to guide students who may be feeling stuck about how to draw interpretations about their observations, but their writing and conversation can certainly go beyond just answering the prompt.

Although any of the action steps above can lead to a student work product, this is often the point where we ask students to connect all the work they have been doing and produce something written or recorded. It can be a reflection paper or a video/photo reflection or any other creative work product.

To help students understand what it means to *make sense* and do interpretive work, you could tell students to include the following:

- Thoughtful reflection and new insights generated
- Descriptions of any relevant experiences/interactions
- Identification and respect for an underlying value or rationale that differs from your own
- Connection to the reading/video/class discussion

You may find it difficult to critique students' writing since it may be very personal. I will provide some grading and evaluation rubrics in the coming pages, but one strategy I want to mention now is to focus on the reflection, not the student. The evaluation of the work then becomes about the student's level of work and thinking and articulation, not the thoughts or feelings themselves. Critiques can be things such as:

- This reflection does not identify a new perspective or viewpoint
- This reflection lacks connection to the reading/topics discussed
- This reflection is missing a discussion of new insights

Using these strategies can help produce more thoughtful work from students.

Make it MATTER

If our goal for study abroad and intercultural experiences is transformative learning, we must help think about and practice applying what they have learned in new contexts. Help students *make it matter* by discussing how to incorporate new knowledge and understanding in their daily lives.

> *Example: Ask students to think about how they will continue to seek awareness about their own culture. Do they have a new mantra or way of looking at things, such as "He who knows others is wise. He who knows himself is enlightened" (Lao Tzu)? How do they hope to incorporate this into their lives?*

The manifestation of this conversation is often beyond the scope of a single class or study abroad experience, so it cannot always be easily assigned or measured. But you can encourage students to think about the ways they can do this and even brainstorm with them.

By helping students think about applying their learning both to familiar contexts (such as being more patient with non-native English speakers in their community) and to unfamiliar contexts (such as exploring new cultural experiences), we can better ensure that the learning from study abroad lasts beyond the experience itself. When students talk about study abroad changing their lives, they often mean it was a memorable experience. For it to be truly transformational, we should encourage them to think not just about how the experience has touched them and what they have learned, but how their learning will impact them moving forward, in future settings and interactions.

Charting Your Course

The PRISM tools described above can be applied to all of the intercultural competence goals you have for students. To demonstrate, I'll now expand on the seven intercultural competence components introduced in Chapter 1. The following PRISM lesson plans recap the learning goal, provide three to four PRISM action steps and specific materials, and offer brief suggestions for utilizing these materials. Many of the *make it relevant* selections are chapters from the books suggested on pages 68 and 69. A cache of additional action steps and materials are provided so that you can mix and match elements, customizing your approach to developing students' intercultural competence.

Cultural Self-Knowledge: Students will articulate insights into their cultural rules and biases.

Learning about our own culture is not always easy. When it comes to our own culture, we find it very hard to identify what makes us similar to other members of our culture and different from people in other cultures. Remember Hofstede's hierarchy of influences: human influences or things we share with everyone, cultural influences or things we share with our cultural group, and personality or individual influences. We need to help students begin to separate universal traits, cultural traits, and personality traits. Particularly in US culture, which promotes individualism, we often like to think of the ways we are different or unique rather than similar to one another. The point of learning about our own culture is raising awareness that we do have a culture—as we tend to think of that as something exotic that other countries have—and beginning to identify what that culture is.

Student Action Steps:

1. Students will *get prepared* by participating in the following warm-up activity:

   Bring to class a short paragraph describing a USA folk hero or role model. Share with the class the attributes that make these individuals admirable.

   Folk heroes are such a part of our common knowledge and lore that we do not stop to think about ***why*** *they became a part of our history. Just a quick discussion about traits that have been deemed admirable in our history is quite revealing and can provide insights into what we share as a national culture, both in terms of history and in terms of values. Students may find contradictions between traits in heroes, or they may find that what was once admirable is no longer so, and this is an important part of the discovery too—that cultures change over time and that people within a culture are not identical when it comes to what they value.*
2. Students will *get involved* in conversations to explore their own cultural rules and biases by completing the following assignment:

   Ask a few locals how they perceive visitors from the USA. What assumptions do they have about people from the USA?

   Students may find this to be a very awkward topic to raise with strangers, who would likely hesitate to be critical. But when approached in a spirit of true curiosity, students find this to be an insightful and informative conversation.
3. Students will *make sense* of their own cultural rules and biases through class discussion and writing, considering the following prompt:

What have you discovered is part of USA culture that you had not realized before? What did you think was just "normal" that is actually cultural? How does this help you better understand the nature of culture in general and USA culture in particular?

When students do a make sense *exercise they should begin to bring in some of the learning from the previous action steps as well as any informal learning. The prompts are to guide students who may be feeling stuck about how to draw interpretations about their observations, but their writing and conversation can certainly go beyond just answering the prompt.*

PRISM Additional Resources: Cultural Self-Knowledge	
Get PREPARED	**Quotes for Conversation** "Everything that irritates us about others can lead us to an understanding of ourselves." –Carl Gustav Jung "The final mystery is oneself." –Oscar Wilde "I do think the patriotic thing to do is to critique my country. How else do you make a country better but by pointing out its flaws?" –Bill Maher **Warm-up Activities** Take USA knowledge and values quizzes on *http://GlobalScholar.us* Examine USA proverbs or mottos. Identify the moral or value the proverb or motto is advocating.
Make it RELEVANT	*The Newsroom* 2012. Pilot: "Why America Isn't the Greatest Nation in the World" Available online at https://www.youtube.com/watch?v=1zqOYBabXmA Paige et al., Part I: "You as a culturally diverse person," pp. 39-56. Kohls, Chapter 8: "What makes an American?" pp. 39-43 and Chapter 9: To see ourselves, pp. 45-50. Hess, Section VI: "Exploring Value Systems," 145-162. Miner, Horace Mitchell. "Body Ritual among the Nacirema." *The American Anthropologist*, vol. 58, 1956, 503-507.

Get INVOLVED	**Not American:** Ask one or two locals how they think their country / their citizens are different from citizens of the US. Is it important to them to see themselves in contrast to Americans? Or is it even something they consider?
Make SENSE	How do you think you're different from other people from the USA? How do you think you are similar to other US citizens? What insights does this inquiry give you into US culture? How do you think your culture has shaped you? How has it influenced your values, preferences, and beliefs? Has anyone said something about the US that you found particularly insightful? What about it was insightful? Did it change your thinking about yourself and the US? How?
Make it MATTER	Consider the quote: "I do think the patriotic thing to do is to critique my country. How else do you make a country better but by pointing out its flaws?" –Bill Maher What flaws have you realized about your country that you would like to improve?

Ethnorelative Understanding of Cultural Worldviews: Students will identify the frameworks and elements that underlie and shape the viewpoints of others and respect them without judgment.

Students should focus on the ways individuals are shaped by their culture and deep-level influences. Students should begin to articulate how humans are socialized into a culture and appreciate that different cultures are not better or worse, just different. To adopt an ethnorelative perspective, students need to accept such differences as viable alternatives to their own worldviews.

Student Action Steps:

1. Students will *make it relevant* by reading or watching resources to develop knowledge of ways people are shaped by culture.

   TED Talk by Saba Safdar, "Everything You Always Wanted to Know about Culture"

   Peterson, Part I: What is culture? (15 – 62).

   You may find it helpful to bring in a model, such as the iceberg image or Hofstede's model, to help students picture how cultural influences work.

2. Students will *get involved* in conversations to begin seeing through new viewpoints by doing the following activity:

   Current events: Take a current event (in the US, in your host country, or in the world). Ask a few locals to explain their country's perspective on the issue, as well as how they perceive the American response to the event. What do you think is at the root of these differences?

   This can be approached in a number of different ways, but the point is for students to think about different perspectives on issues as they reflect underlying worldviews and values. If there are not current events of interest, they could explore common issues that all societies face, like homelessness and poverty, alcohol and drug addiction, healthcare, education, and resource allocation.

3. Students will *make sense* of elements important to members of their host culture through class discussion and writing, considering the following prompt:

   What values, historical events, or infrastructures have you discovered that influence the ways people in your host culture behave or structure their lives?

   This prompt is about helping students make connections between the visible and invisible elements of culture. If this feels too broad or dense to students, you can help them identify some visible cultural elements they could examine, such as food choices and meal patterns, styles of dress, architecture and the built environment, or interactional habits.

<table>
<tr><th colspan="2">PRISM Additional Resources: Ethnorelative Understanding of Cultural Worldviews</th></tr>
<tr><td>Get PREPARED</td><td>Quotes for Conversation

“When we understand the needs that motivate our own and others’ behavior, we have no enemies.” —Marshall Rosenberg

“Wherever you go, go with all your heart.” —Confucius

“The real voyage of discovery consists not in seeking new landscapes, but in having new eyes.” —Marcel Proust

“You never really understand a person until you consider things from his point of view . . . until you climb inside of his skin and walk around in it.” —Atticus Finch (Harper Lee)

“We have two ears and one mouth so that we can listen twice as much as we speak.” —Epictetus</td></tr>
<tr><td>Make it RELEVANT</td><td>Thomas and Inkson, Chapter 2: Cultural Knowledge (20–42).

Paige et al., Introduction: “Culture-Learning Strategies” (35-37) and Part II: “Understanding the Ways Cultures Can Differ in Values” (59 - 65).

Kohls, Chapter 6: “Culture Defined” (25-30) and Chapter 7: “Comparing and Contrasting Culture” (31-38).

Hess, Chapter 1: “Culture Learning” (3-10) and Chapter 2: “Attitudes and Character Traits that Promote Cultural Learning” (11 - 20).</td></tr>
<tr><td>Get INVOLVED</td><td>Legal-unease: Visit with a few locals about any laws you find interesting, different, or strange. Can they explain the philosophy or reasoning behind the law? How do they feel about the law? Did you learn more about their values through exploring this law?</td></tr>
</table>

Make SENSE	How do people where you are studying abroad engage issues of justice, health, sustainability, and peace? What values and beliefs might influence how and why they address these issues in this way? How do you balance openness and cultural respect with strength of identity (being true to yourself)?
Make it MATTER	Contemplate the statement, "We go abroad not just to see different things, but to see things differently." Does this reflect your experience abroad? How will you utilize this approach in the future?

Culture-Specific Knowledge: Students will articulate habits, norms, and values typical of members of another culture.

As students identify differences between the host culture and their own, it is helpful to guide them to connect those differences to environmental, historical, religious, political, or economic factors. For example, if students in Spain notice a preference for ham and pork products, ask them to investigate this more: can they connect historical settlements and religious norms of Christians, Jews, and Muslims to this food preference? Students should also begin to recognize that there are many components (beyond national culture) which influene the people of their host culture, and there are many differences within their host culture.

Student Action Steps:

1. Student will *make it relevant* by reading or watching resources to develop knowledge of elements important to members of their host culture.

   Read *CultureGrams™* for your country.

   The World Edition Individual Reports *published by CultureGrams™, https://www.culturegrams.com/, are concise readings describing daily life and culture, including customs and norms, history, political structure, important economic features, and more. Easy to read, up to date, and relevant, these readings provide both broad information and specific tips like greetings, gift-giving norms, and taboos.*

2. Students will *get involved* in conversations about elements important to members of their host culture by doing the following activity:

   Ask one or two locals: What are some things that make you proud of your country/city/region, or proud to be a _____ (Spaniard, Brit, etc.)?

   This is a particularly useful assignment because it often helps students to see that something they may have thought of as unimportant or even irritating is of value to others. Students may also find that the person they interview struggles with the notion of pride in the US sense, so this exercise serves a dual purpose of helping them be self-reflective about the cultural concept of pride.

3. Students will *make sense* of elements important to members of their host culture through class discussion and writing, considering the following prompt:

   What are the habits of the locals? Are there environmental, physical, cultural, or other reasons that they engage in those habits? Have you tried to emulate those habits, and what was that experience like?

   An important part of any conversation on cultural frameworks is keeping observations and generalizations from becoming stereotypes and simplistic answers. The goal is for students to connect observations they have about behaviors to underlying values and motivations, and to treat those underlying values and motivations with respect.

PRISM Additional Resources: Culture-Specific Information	
Get PREPARED	**Quotes for Conversation** "When you travel, remember that a foreign country is not designed to make you comfortable. It is designed to make its own people comfortable." –Clifton Fadiman "You don't get harmony when everybody sings the same note." –Doug Floyd **Warm-up Activities** Learn more about cultural encounters on *http://GlobalScholar.us*

Make it RELEVANT	*Global Road Warriors,* Available at https://www.globalroadwarrior.com/ *Culture Crossing Guide,* http://guide.culturecrossing.net/ *Speak the Culture* series by Andrew Whittaker Resources page under the Culture section of http://GlobalScholar.us for country-specific readings Denslow, Lanie. *Worldwise.* NY Fairchild Publications, 2006.
Get INVOLVED	**Iconic Image:** Consider a popular or iconic site in your host city. Ask one or two locals: what makes this special to you? What do tourists not understand about this? **Local Environment:** Interview a few locals, and ask them to describe the native plants, trees, vegetation, and wildlife. What do they appreciate about these things? How do these things contribute to the local life and economy? How do people nurture/protect the environment? How does their knowledge of and approach to the environment differ from that of the typical American? **Folk hero:** Ask one or two locals: who is a famous folk hero? What is this person's legend or story? What do you think he/she represents? On your own: research this person. What values do you think he/she portrays that resonate with the people in your host culture?
Make SENSE	What is daily life like for the people in your host culture? What joys and challenges do they say they experience? How is it different from life in the United States? Consider ways you think people in your host culture behave that are confusing or contradictory. Delve deeper: what factors might play into this—historical, religious, environmental, class, personality?
Make it MATTER	Contemplate the statement, "When you meet people, show real appreciation, then genuine curiosity" (Martha Beck). Does this reflect your experience abroad? How will you utilize this approach in the future?

Empathy and Respect: Students will demonstrate an ability to interpret intercultural experiences from the perspectives of more than one worldview and recognize the feelings of another cultural group.

While we often find it easy to empathize when we are not impacted by the other person's perspective, it is difficult to empathize when it means we have to acknowledge how we might have to change, or when we need to give credence to two differing opinions at the same time. When we talk about challenging students to develop empathy, we are asking them to see another perspective *particularly* when it challenges their own.

Student Action Steps:

1. Students will *get prepared* by participating in class discussion that explores empathy as it relates to the following quote:

   "I don't like that man. I must get to know him more."
   —Abraham Lincoln

   Once, in class, I defined discrimination as ascribing negative characteristics to a group of people you do not know very well. A student asked, "What is it called when you ascribe negative characteristics to a group of people you DO know well?" My answer is: a lack of empathy. Empathy challenges students to continually seek to learn more about others' perspectives. It does not mean you need to embrace those perspectives yourself, but that you begin to understand and release judgment and negativity.

2. Students will *make it relevant* by reading or watching resources to begin understanding how to be empathetic.

   Richards, Sam. 2010. "A radical experiment in empathy. TEDxPSU." https://www.youtube.com/watch?v=kUEGHd-QO7WA

   This is a fascinating and provocative TED talk. As the title says, it is a radical experiment. Students may feel it is an attack on the US military or that it portrays a simplistic overgeneralization, and to a certain degree, that is what makes it an excellent starting point for conversation. Ask students, "Are there people in the world who believe the things he says? Can you, through his storytelling, understand why they believe these things? Can you recognize that there may be perspectives you hold which are equally unfair and offensive to someone else?"

3. Students will *get involved* in conversations and storytelling from a different point of view, and students will *make sense* of their challenges and successes in being empathetic.

   Encourage students to think about an emotional or frustrating encounter, and retell the story from the other person's point of view. The "Change Your LENS" exercise below models this in a step-by-step process.

PRISM Additional Resources: Empathy and Respect	
Get PREPARED	**Quotes for Conversation** "True empathy requires you step outside your own emotions to view things entirely from the perspective of the other person." —Anonymous "Empathy is seeing with the eyes of another, listening with the ears of another, and feeling with the heart of another." —Alfred Adler "Empathy is about standing in someone else's shoes, feeling with his or her heart, seeing with his or her eyes." —Daniel Pink
Make it RELEVANT	Rifkin, Jeremy. (2010). RSA Animate: The Empathic Civilisation. https://www.youtube.com/watch?v=l7AWnfFRc7gand-feature=youtu.be. Thomas and Inkson, Ch. 3: Mindfulness and Cross-Cultural Skills (43–62). LeBaron, Michelle and Venashri Pillary. Chapter 6: Capacities and skills for intercultural conflict resolution. Conflict Across Cultures (111–135). Boston: Intercultural Press, 2006. De Waal, Frans. Chapter 7: Crooked timber. The Age of Empathy (201–225). New York: Harmony Books, 2009. Calloway-Thomas, Carolyn. Chapter 1: A Global Imperative: The unveiling of empathy. Empathy in a Global World (1–24). Thousand Oaks, CA: Sage Publications, 2010.

Make it RELEVANT (continued)	Ehrlich, Paul R. and Ornstein, Robert. E. Chapter 8: Getting to 'alike' one another. Humanity on a Tightrope: Thoughts on Empathy, Family, and Big Changes for a Viable Future (103-116). Blue Ridge Summit, PA: Rowman and Littlefield Publishers, 2010. Hoffman, Martin L. Chapter 8: Empathy's limitations: Over-arousal and bias, and Chapter 12: The universality and culture issue. Empathy and Moral Development: Implications for Caring and Justice (197–298 and 273–285). Cambridge: University Press, 2000.
Get INVOLVED	Interview one or two locals about how they respond to others in need. How do they help family, friends, and strangers in need? What prompts them to help others? What kinds of goods, services, or monetary amounts are they willing to give? How does this differ from US approaches to assistance?
Make SENSE	In what ways have you been impacted by listening to others' stories? How have you changed your way of thinking?
Make it MATTER	Discuss how to incorporate new knowledge and understanding in your daily lives. Do the words of wisdom, *"Empathize before you analyze!"* (Kate Nasser) resonate in a new way?

Sociolinguistic Awareness and Intercultural Communication Skills: Students will articulate a complex understanding of cultural differences in verbal and nonverbal communication and be able to skillfully negotiate a shared understanding that bridges those differences.

For many students, the largest concern of communicating while abroad is the language itself, but this is only a small part of communication. Students need to learn about the many elements of communication that carry different meanings and vary across cultures, and practice using those methods.

Student Action Steps:

1. Students will *get prepared* for intercultural communication by participating in the class activity Barnga.

   Barnga is a classic simulation game modeling intercultural communication. This card game allows participants to experience what it's like to be in an environment where their assumptions about the operating rules differ but they don't realize it. For full instructions about leading the simulation, see the book *Barnga* by Sivasailam Thiagarajan (published by Intercultural Press).

2. Students will *get involved* in conversations about communication differences.

   Market Interactions: Go to the market, a store, or a restaurant. Observe how locals interact with vendors: what are greeting forms? Who initiates the interaction? How does the customer ask for something different? Does price negotiation occur? How do interactions conclude? Practice modeling these styles. What was the experience like?

   This is an activity in which you can give students a lot of freedom to engage with the barista at their favorite coffee shop or the vendors at local markets. Learning to observe and describe differences is a great way to interrupt patterned models of behavior and learn more about cultural differences in interaction and communication.

3. Students will *make sense* of communication differences in another culture through written work and class discussion.

   Ask students to dissect a miscommunication using the "What do they MEAN?" approach.

   In Chapter 1 I briefly introduced the "What do they MEAN" method. It's a helpful tool to look at again, as it is not always easy to identify communication differences. We tend to report our interpretation (i.e., he's rude, she's snobby) and not the communication element (i.e., he spoke loudly, she didn't respond to me). To begin to examine why we have different interpretations, we have to start with the elements of communication and see if the meanings we attach to these are the same or different from those the other person perceives. To do this, think about an interaction or conversation you've had where you had a misunderstanding or a negative outcome. Consider the "What do they MEAN" elements of communication and what meaning you attach to each. Then explore with locals whether your interpretations are the same as theirs.

PRISM Additional Resources: Sociolinguistic Awareness and Intercultural Communication Skills	
Get PREPARED	**Quotes for Conversation** "The most important thing in communication is to hear what isn't being said." —Peter Drucker "To effectively communicate, we must realize that we are all different in the way we perceive the world and use this understanding as a guide to our communication with others." —Anthony Robbins "The single biggest problem in communication is the illusion that it has taken place." —George Bernard Shaw **Warm-up Activities** Activities from *52 Activities for Improving Cross-Cultural Communication*, by Donna M. Stringer and Patricia A. Cassiday. (2009). Intercultural Press. Think about a person who strikes you as: "rude," "insincere," "gruff," "blunt." What about their language reinforces your negative perception of that person? Are there other possible meanings behind their language choices?
Make it RELEVANT	Thomas and Inkson, Ch. 5: "Communicating, Negotiating, and Resolving Conflict" (84–106). Paige et al., Part VI: "Strategies for Intercultural Communication (121–124), Part VII: Non-Verbal Communication" (129–138). Kohls, Chapter 17: "A Handy Guide to Intercultural Communication" (83–89). Nolan, Riall. Chapter 3: "Communication and Culture, Chapter 4 and Verbal Communication, Chapter 5: Nonverbal Communication." *Communicating and Adapting Across Cultures* (33–59). Westport, CT: Bergin and Garve, 1999.

Get INVOLVED	**Expressions:** Think about a new motto, phrase, or word that you've heard used. Ask or confirm with one or two locals: what does it mean? How is it used? Is there a popular/historical/cultural basis for its usage? Do they notice when non-native speakers use it or misuse it?
Make SENSE	Describe a time you offended someone. What did you do wrong? Did the situation escalate because you continued to use US styles and norms, rather than culturally appropriate ones? Describe differences in gestures, body posture, use of space, use of silence, use of directness, and/or use of politeness, and what those differences communicate. How has learning the language, dialect, and communication style affected you?
Make it MATTER	Consider the statement, "Communication works for those who work at it" (John Powell). How will you use the skills you've developed in future communication?

Curiosity and Discovery: Students will demonstrate an ability to ask complex questions about other cultures, and seek out and articulate answers to these questions that reflect multiple cultural perspectives.

Curiosity is one of those traits that we all want to see in students but may not know how to facilitate. Embedded in this learning objective are a couple of ways to do this. One is teaching them to ***ask*** questions, which can come in the form of encouraging students to examine with new eyes or just simply to question everything with a desire to learn more. Another is teaching them to look for complexity, or encouraging them to seek deeper-level knowledge; in other words, not just to ask questions but to ask ***complex*** questions. Last is teaching them articulate multiple perspectives. As you guide students to develop curiosity, these prompts—*what* is different, *why* is it different, *how* do others see it—may help.

Student Action Steps:

1. Students will *get prepared* to be curious by completing the activity: create a list of five open-ended questions that you could ask people

in your host culture.

This exercise has the dual purpose of helping students begin learning about what they may find in their host cultures and begin thinking about ways to frame questions.

2. Students will *make it relevant* by reading or watching resources exploring how to be curious.

   Read selections from Isay, D. (2007). *Listening is an Act of Love: A Celebration of American Life from the StoryCorps Project.* NY: Penguin Books.

   The StoryCorps project is an initiative to record oral histories of everyday people. Using this text in an intercultural learning setting has a dual purpose. First, it portrays a range of stories and perspectives that can teach students about people they might never otherwise meet and learn about. Because the stories are all recorded by a family member or friend, they reveal an honesty and poignancy that engenders great respect. The stories inform students about different lives and experiences and even challenge their assumptions about people different from them.

   Second, it can model for students how to learn about someone else's story, and how to be curious in respectful ways. They even provide a list of great questions to ask: https://storycorps.org/great-questions/.

   Listening is an Act of Love *was the first book published by StoryCorps, but several others have been published since then, and you can also hear the stories online at https://storycorps.org/.*

3. Students will *make sense* of the results of their exploration by articulating new, multifaceted understandings, responding to the prompt: "Wisdom begins in wonder." —Socrates.

PRISM Additional Resources: Curiosity and Discovery	
Get PREPARED	**Quotes for Conversation** "The cure for boredom is curiosity. There is no cure for curiosity." –Ellen Parr "Develop a passion for learning. If you do, you will never cease to grow." –Anthony J. D'Angelo "Curiosity is one of the great secrets of happiness." –Bryant McGill

Get PREPARED (continued)	**Warm-up Activities** Think about a topic that you know very little about but that has piqued your interest. What do you find intriguing about it? What else do you want to learn about it? If you met someone who was an expert on that topic, what kinds of things would you ask him or her?
Make it RELEVANT	Wesch, M. (2010). *TEDxNYED Presents Michael Wesch.* TEDxNYED. https://www.youtube.com/watch?v=DwyCA-tyNYHw Davies, Aled. (2011). *How to be Curious in a Difficult Conversation.* https://www.youtube.com/watch?v=NABSprZKGeM Kashdan, Todd. Chapter 4: "The Curious Moment" (59–90) and Chapter 7: "The Anxious Mind and the Curious Spirit" (167–208). *Curious? Discover the Missing Ingredient to a Fulfilling Life.* New York: HarperCollins, 2009. Barell, John. Chapter 2: "Models of Inquiry" (20–38) and Chapter 4: "The Nature of Good Questions" (59–78). *Developing More Curious Minds.* Alexandria, VA: Association for Supervision and Curriculum Development, 2003. Gibbs, Cheryl and Warhover, Tom. Chapter 9: "Observation, Curiosity, and Note-Taking." *Getting the Whole Story: Reporting and Writing the News* (208–222). New York: The Guilford Press, 2002. Laing, R. D. (1971). "There Is Something I Don't Know." *Knots.* Ringwood, Victoria: Penguin, 1971.
Get INVOLVED	**Graffiti:** Find some sort of graffiti or a popular poster on the street. Ask one or two locals what it means, how long it has been there, what it represents/stands for, and/or why they think it is placed there. Ask whether graffiti is considered vandalism or street art. **Get someone's story:** Have an in-depth conversation with someone you've met while abroad (conversation partner, host family member, friend), and try to discover something new. Use some of the following question lists for ideas: http://www.intlcenter.org/conversation.html https://storycorps.org/great-questions/

Make SENSE	Is there something about your host culture you would like to better understand? How can you find out more about it? What is the hardest thing about being curious? Why do you think it is difficult to be curious? How can you work on this?
Make it MATTER	Consider the following: There is always something more to learn. How will you keep learning?

Openness and Flexibility: Students will demonstrate an ability to seek out interactions with different people and practice new, culturally appropriate behaviors.

While it may seem that students who are choosing to study abroad are people who already have the skillset of openness, there is a big difference between openness to new experiences and openness to change. With this learning goal, we are pushing students to be open to change, whether it is change in thoughts or behavior. To change thoughts, we must be open to hearing perspectives that seem radical; to change behaviors, we must be open to making mistakes. Being open to change requires effort, thought, vulnerability, and especially a willingness to be in situations that are unfamiliar or uncomfortable—but the outcome of this openness is truly transformational learning.

Student Action Steps:

1. Students will *get prepared* for openness by participating in a class discussion based on the following quote:

   "The measure of intelligence is the ability to change."

   —Albert Einstein

   For many, being open can feel like being wishy-washy, or perhaps worse, being wrong. Framing the concept of openness as a measure of intelligence can make it less threatening.

2. Students will *make it relevant* by reading or watching resources exploring how to be open.

   The Upside of Failure: TEDxKids@SMU Talk by Sadie Funk

This is a fantastic personal narrative from a former Peace Corps Volunteer not only about trying and failing, but about seeking out and respecting local perspectives.

3. Students will *get involved* by practicing openness with locals and will *make sense* of their experience of suspending judgment of others through reflection.

   New Experience: Go to a ceremony, rite, celebration, event, or activity—it can be religious, sports oriented, or cultural in nature. What did you find uncomfortable about the experience? What did you learn that surprised you?

   Again, while many study abroad students seem to gravitate toward new experiences, they may primarily seek out activities that are fun, not necessarily uncomfortable. Anything new can lead to learning, but the more they put themselves in uncomfortable, unfamiliar situations, the more they are challenged to be open and the more they can potentially learn.

PRISM Additional Resources: Openness and Flexibility	
Get PREPARED	**Quotes for Conversation** "It's good to do uncomfortable things. It's weight training for life." –Anne Lamott "Remember, there are no mistakes, only lessons." –Cherie-Carter Scott "Ever tried. Ever failed. No matter. Try again. Fail again. Fail better." –Samuel Beckett **Warm-up Activities** Assess your intercultural sensitivity - *Maximizing Study Abroad: A Students' Guide to Strategies for Language and Culture Learning and Use. http://www.globaled.us/plato/maxsa.html* Do the cultural learning strategies inventory - *Maximizing Study Abroad: A Students' Guide to Strategies for Language and Culture Learning and Use. http://www.globaled.us/plato/maxsa.html*
Make it RELEVANT	LeBaron, Michelle and Pillay, Venashri. Chapter 6: "Capacities and Skills for Intercultural Conflict Resolution." *Conflict across Cultures: A Unique Experience of Bridging Differences* (111-136). Boston, MA: Nicholas Brealey Publishing, 2006.

Make it RELEVANT (continued)	Nolan, Riall. Chapter 2: "Encountering Difference." *Communicating and Adapting Across Cultures* (13–32). Westport, CT: Bergin and Garvey, 1999. Wagner, Kenneth and Tony Magistrale. Chapter 6: "Cultural Change and Personal Discovery." *Writing Across Culture* (129–146). New York: Peter Lang, 1995. Paige et al, "Continue the Learning" (143–159).[i]
Make SENSE	Describe a time you stretched yourself. What did you do, and why was this a new experience for you? What skills and qualities did you practice? How did this impact you, and how do you think it will impact you in the future? What have you had the most trouble adapting to? Have you finally adapted to it, or do you believe you'll never adapt to it? Think about a time when things did not go the way you planned. How did you respond to the situation? What skills and characteristics did you learn/develop/hone? Describe something new you tried: a food completely outside your comfort zone, a new form of transportation, a habit or activity. Did you enjoy the experience of trying something new? To what degree do you want to assimilate into the local culture? Why or why not?
Make it MATTER	Consider the quote "It is never too late to give up our prejudices" (Henry David Thoreau). What prejudices do you want to work on giving up?

Measuring the Student Product

At some point, you may expect a student product: a written essay, a photographic journal, or a call-to-action video. The student output, whether it is written, oral, or visual, is an excellent opportunity for students to showcase their learning. Such products often tend to be very personal, though, making the process challenging for both students and faculty, particularly if it is graded. Students may resist opening themselves up, sharing personal thoughts and feelings, or revealing mistakes, and may feel personally criticized by the grading process. Faculty may find it challenging to objectively grade subjective material, and may find the process time-consuming. One alternative is to simply give credit for completion, but even if you do this, it is still useful to have a framework for yourself and for students to identify quality work and markers of learning, and to utilize descriptors or language to push students to higher levels of development.

One approach is to adapt the AAC&U VALUE Rubric on Intercultural Knowledge and Competence, which, as explained in Chapter 1, provides a benchmark, two milestones, and a capstone measure for each of the six dimensions it identifies. This means that you would have a different rubric for each aspect of intercultural competence. These could line up very nicely if you use many or all of the AAC&U's aspects of intercultural competence as your learning outcomes. To use this approach, for example, you could have a "Make Sense" reflective writing assignment for Knowledge of Cultural Frameworks or for Empathy, and then evaluate the student work using the AAC&U rubric.

Another approach is to design a single rubric that can measure multiple student artifacts. The benefit of this is that it simplifies measurements (for both you and the student), and you have the opportunity to see change and growth from the first assignment to the last. As I looked to build such a rubric, I consulted reflective learning models such as Hatton and Smith 1995, Moon 2004, and Smith 2011. These models encourage students to move from simple description to deeper interpretation and analysis. They also encourage students to look at experiences through alternative viewpoints and to develop conclusions, and they suggest future action. According to these models, some markers of growth and learning include:

- Self-questioning, self-development, challenging of one's own ideas and behaviors
- Taking into account others' points of view
- Displaying curiosity and wonder about things unknown

- Exploring impact of emotions and looking for ways to "step back" from emotions
- Moving beyond simple description to making meaning
- Building theory or understanding from observations

As I looked at these makers and my learning outcomes for students, I identified two sets of expectations: understanding/explaining, and valuing/appreciating difference. You can see these two expectations in the three learning outcomes I created.

1. Students will demonstrate **cultural self-awareness** by understanding specific norms and values in their own culture, appreciating the ways those norms and values are seen from other perspectives, and explaining cultural roots.
2. Students will demonstrate **awareness of other cultures** by understanding specific cultural norms and values, and valuing and explaining the positive aspects of cultural differences.
3. Students will demonstrate **competencies for appropriate and effective interaction models** by understanding specific communication differences, showing a desire to respond in appropriate ways and an ability to interact effectively.

How does this look in reflective writing or other interpretive assignments? Drawing upon reflective learning markers, I developed the following metrics. The manifestation of understanding and explaining is moving beyond simple description to making meaning and building theory or understandings from observations. The manifestation of valuing and appreciating difference is taking into account other points of view and self-questioning.

In the rubric on the following page, I describe in more depth the markers for levels of understanding and explaining and valuing and appreciating difference. These descriptors can help you more objectively respond to students' work products and provide specific feedback on how students can improve.

	1: Observation	2: Growing Awareness	3: Appreciation and Eagerness	4: Emerging Comprehension	5: Intercultural Consciousness
	Failure to address important elements	Lacking important elements	Average	Very good	Exemplary
Demonstrates insights and revelations **(understands and explains)**	The reflection is simply descriptive. The reflection does not attempt to understand, explore, or make meaning of experiences or observations and does not connect to the reading.	The reflection is mostly descriptive but may show basic attempts to understand or learn more about observations. The reflection may mention the reading but does not make connections.	The reflection begins to make simple interpretations. The reflection may list simple new understandings or simplistic personal growth and change. The reflection demonstrates an emerging desire to learn or sense of wonder. The reflection may offer a quote from the reading but does not connect meaningfully.	The reflection attempts to articulate more in-depth interpretations. The reflection describes revelations about self and culture though it may reveal inconsistency. The reflection demonstrates an increasing desire to learn and may list ways knowledge is incomplete. The reflection attempts to connect the reading but falls short of level 5.	The reflection shows complex interpretations and deep, thoughtful insights about self and culture and discusses how to apply learning. The reflection shows a strong desire to learn more and may offer ideas for gaining more knowledge. The reflection draws thoughtful conclusions by connecting to the readings in meaningful ways.
Interprets and views from multiple perspectives **(values and appreciates difference)**	The reflection does not recognize other points of view or is not able to suspend judgment of the other. The reflection may be critical or negative toward the other.	The reflection begins to recognize other points of view but is simplistic and superficial, and prefers own perspective; lists personal experience with the other through a single perspective.	The reflection shows increasing recognition of other points of view and shows growing respect for differences. The reflection begins to validate differences or attempts simple explanations of differences.	The reflection describes and respects other perspectives in more depth but may not reach level 5. The reflection attempts to explain differences in more depth, or draw thoughtful connections and conclusions without fully exploring them.	The reflection describes other perspectives in considerable depth and recognizes and respects the complexity of culture. The reflection draws thoughtful conclusions and may describe an incident through the other's point of view.

Tailoring the PRISM for Your Students

The instructional goals, tools, specific materials, and approaches for assigning and measuring student work described in previous chapters should enable you to build a course that suits your instructional style and your students—and to be as creative as you like.

I have used these components in a variety of ways, including creating a one-credit course focused solely on intercultural learning. My course uses three learning outcomes, four of the five PRISM tools throughout the course, and the fifth PRISM tool for the final assignment.

You could choose to integrate a few intercultural learning outcomes into a course you teach abroad and use some of the PRISM learning tools to supplement or replace some of the approaches you would use if teaching the course on campus.

Or you could adapt the PRISM learning tools for your class abroad by integrating your discipline-specific learning goals with intercultural learning goals. For example, if you are teaching a political science class, you could design PRISM activities that incorporate intercultural learning with political science concepts.

Finally, of course, you could teach a course like mine that is wholly focused on intercultural learning. The syllabus is in Appendix A.

You can also incorporate the PRISM outside of a class-based structure. Appendix B covers a number of ways to use these tools in study abroad programming that is not class-based.

Finally, you can share the strategies directly with your students. One of the goals of the PRISM model is to have students learn to be learners, and showing them the processes and goals can be very productive. Appendix C provides some handouts that can be shared with students to help them understand the transformative learning approach of the PRISM and their role in applying it.

Conclusion

The pedagogy of the PRISM provides a flexible, holistic framework to organize and deliver intercultural learning content and engage students in study abroad experiences, and I hope that it inspires your own creative ideas for implementing and applying it. Coupling your own intercultural experiences and academic background with the content and tools here, you can help students derive meaning from their experiences and apply their learning in deep and significant ways.

Study abroad can lead to rich learning opportunities, but we must move beyond assuming learning happens through mere exposure and competence happens through trial and error. As educators, we know that we have a role to play in guiding, directing, and shaping that learning and competence, and through the content of the book you now have the content and tools necessary to facilitate that.

As we provide more opportunities to prepare, relate, involve, make sense of, and make cultural learning experiences matter, we can help students have more nuanced, multifaceted experiences and understandings. In doing so, we can create the transformative learning experiences that will lead to interculturally competent students.

APPENDIX A

Making it Work:
Syllabus for One-Credit-Hour Course

Course Description

The class enhances the study abroad experience by providing opportunities, guidance, and structure for learning *outside* the classroom, in the study abroad locale. Specifically, it gives you chances to interact with your study abroad community, and to reflect upon and process your experiences as you cross cultures.

This course is about *you* making sense of your experience and framing it in broader, intercultural competence terms. It is about *you* making the most of your time abroad to explore, experience, and learn. The readings, assignments, and reflections are like compass points, giving you direction but allowing you to do your own learning.

Upon completion of the course, you should be able to:

- Discuss the nature of culture and its influences
- Describe skills developed, such as empathy and intercultural communication skills
- Describe your own intercultural interactions non-judgmentally

Learning Outcomes

1. Students will demonstrate **cultural self-awareness** by understanding specific cultural norms and values, appreciating the ways those norms and values are seen from other perspectives, and explaining cultural roots.

2. Students will demonstrate **awareness of other cultures by** understanding specific cultural norms and values, and valuing and explaining the positive aspects of cultural differences.
3. Students will demonstrate **competencies for appropriate and effective interaction models** by understanding specific communication differences, showing a desire to respond in appropriate ways and an ability to interact effectively.

Course Materials

Cultural Intelligence: Living and Working Globally by David C. Thomas and Kerr Inkson (available through Amazon.com, Barnes & Noble, and other bookshops)

CultureGrams™ for your country

Various readings to download from D2L

Course Policies and Expectations

- Class time is condensed and limited to the orientation and midterm visits. Students must attend a majority of the activities with the faculty member and contribute to the discussion. Students are expected to arrive to events on time, be attentive, and participate in activities and discussions.
- Email and D2L will be utilized throughout the semester to distribute information, make announcements, and to inform students of situations related to the class. Each student is responsible for frequently checking his or her email through the TCU email system.
- Students are expected to read and conform to the Academic Conduct Policy found in the TCU Student Handbook.

Evaluation Criteria

Local Learning Activities: Take advantage of the many opportunities offered by your program and throughout your city. Approved activities must be of a culturally academic nature and should not be something you are doing for another course. Examples include:

- Program-organized activities
- Local organized activity (lecture, guided tour)

4 activities, 5 points each = 20 points

PRISM Assignments: PRISM assignments allow you to explore a component of intercultural competency in more depth. There will be a short reading assignment and an assignment that requires interaction in the community. You need to complete the interaction activity and then write a 350- to 500-word reflection that **incorporates your personal experience and the reading**. I will be looking for:

- Summary of the experience
- Thoughtful reflection and new insights generated
- Identification and respect for an underlying value or rationale that differs from your own
- Connection to the reading (citation)
- Grammar and overall quality of writing

4 assignments, 10 points each = 40 points

Change your LENS: There will be a number of times you will have an "aha" moment of enlightenment. These might be interactions of frustration and outrage or positivity and awe. Write about one of these following the "Change Your LENS" model. 10 points

FINAL: Make it Matter: Your final reflection should be a summary of what you've learned on the topics of intercultural competence and global citizenship, and what you want to do next. Assignments will be graded on your ability to connect experiences to cultural and global learning, your ability to connect personal experiences to readings, and the quality of thought and reflection in the paper. Grammar and overall quality of writing will also be considered. 20 points

Evaluation Rubric

Evaluation Criteria	Potential Points	Total Points
Local Learning	4 @ 5 points each	20
PRISM Assignments	5 @ 10 points each	50
Change Your LENS	1 @ 10 points each	10
Final	20 points	20
		100

AMERICAN INFLUENCES IN A GLOBAL WORLD

Get Prepared: *"It is not my place to doubt the sincere beliefs of others. My job is to question my own beliefs." —Jonathan Lockwood Huie*

Learning Goals:

a. Explore the ways the US has not only a presence but an influence in your host country.

b. Explain the values that underlie US normative culture.

Make it Relevant:

Read Chapter 8: Developing Cultural Intelligence in a Global World.

Get Involved:

Do one of the following activities:

Concepts of Americans
Ask one or two locals how they perceive Americans. What assumptions do they have about American people?

OR

Not American
Ask one or two locals how they think their country/their citizens are

Course Schedule

Week	READING	ASSIGNMENT
Pre-departure - Arrival Week	Ch. 1: "Living and Working in the Global Village"	Attend Orientation Activities
1	Ch. 8: "Developing Cultural Intelligence in a Global World"	*ENGAGEMENT ASSIGNMENT:* American influences
2	Ch. 2: "Cultural Knowledge"	
3	Global Road Warrior for your country (Overview, Country Facts, Society, and Culture) and *CultureGrams*^{TM} for your country	*ENGAGEMENT ASSIGNMENT:* Host Country Values
4	Ch. 3: "Mindfulness and Cross-Cultural Skills"	*ENGAGEMENT ASSIGNMENT:* Engagement Skills
5	Ch. 5: "Communicating, Negotiating, and Resolving Conflict"	*ENGAGEMENT ASSIGNMENT:* Intercultural Communication Skills
6	A Single Lucid Moment - http://www.peacecorps.gov/volunteer/learn/whatlike/ownwords/1229/	Attend midterm activities
7	Ch. 4: "Making Decisions across Cultures"	*A-HA REVELATION*
8	Conclusion: "The Essentials of Cultural Intelligence"	*FINAL REFLECTION*

different from Americans. To what degree do they want to distinguish themselves from Americans? Is it even something they consider?

OR

Current events
Consider an event currently taking place in the US. Ask one or two locals how they perceive the American response to the event. How do they think they might respond differently in their country? What do you think is at the root of these differences?

Make Sense:

Write a 350- to 500-word essay, summarizing your discoveries from the interaction and reflecting on one or more of the following questions:

What have you discovered is part of American culture that you had not realized before? What did you think was just "normal" that is actually cultural?

How do you think culture shapes people? How has it influenced your values, preferences, and beliefs?

Consider the ways you see the presence of the United States (media, products, etc.) in your host country. In what ways do you think this influences how locals perceive US Americans?

HOST COUNTRY VALUES

Get Prepared: "When I am able to resist the temptation to judge others, I can see them as teachers." —Gerald Jampolsky

Learning Goals:

a. Explore the underlying values of your host culture.
b. Develop awareness of the diversity within individuals.

Make it Relevant:

Read Chapter 2: "Cultural Knowledge."

Get Involved:

Do one of the following activities:

Folk hero
Ask one or two locals: Who is a famous folk hero? What is this person's legend or story? What do you think he/she represents? On your own, research this person: What values do you think he/she portrays that resonate with the people in your host culture?

OR

Local Pride
Ask one or two locals: What are some things that make you proud of your country/city/region, or proud to be a _____ (Spaniard, Brit, etc.)?

OR

Iconic Image
Consider a popular or iconic site in your host city. Ask one or two locals: What makes this special to you? What do tourists not understand about this?

Make Sense:

Write a 350- to 500-word essay summarizing your discoveries from the interaction and reflecting on one or more of the following questions:

> What are you discovering to be some primary differences between life at home and life in your host city? Do you find these differences frustrating, or intriguing? What do you think are the reasons driving these differences?
>
> To what degree do you want to assimilate into the local culture? In order to do so, what do you think you'll have to do / change / understand? Does assimilating into the local culture mean losing your own identity? What parts?
>
> What have you had the most trouble adapting to? Why? How important is it to you to adapt or not adapt?

ENGAGEMENT SKILLS

Get Prepared: *"Empathy is seeing with the eyes of another, listening with the ears of another, and feeling with the heart of another."* —Alfred Adler

Learning Goals:

a. Practice empathy, flexibility, and curiosity.
b. Become aware of the ways your cultural training influences you.

Make it Relevant:

Read Chapter 3: Mindfulness and Cross-Cultural Skills.

Get Involved:

Do one of the following activities:

New Experience
Go to a ceremony, rite, celebration, event, or activity—it can be religious, a sports event, or cultural in nature. What did you find uncomfortable about the experience? What did you learn that surprised you?

OR

Graffiti
Find some sort of graffiti or a popular poster on the street. Ask one or two locals what it means, how long it has been there, what it represents or stands for, and/or why they think it is placed there. Ask whether graffiti is considered vandalism or street art.

OR

In-depth Insights
Have an in-depth conversation with someone you've met while abroad (conversation partner, host family member, friend), and try to learn about something that doesn't make sense to you or that you can't relate to.

Make Sense:

Write a 350- to 500-word essay, summarizing your discoveries from the interaction and reflecting on one or more of the following questions:

What stereotypes—yours and theirs—were challenged in this exchange?

How do you balance cultural respect with strength of identity (being true to yourself)?

What is the hardest thing about being empathetic, curious, or open? How can you work on this?

INTERCULTURAL COMMUNICATION SKILLS

Get Prepared: *"The most important thing in communication is to hear what isn't being said."* —Peter Drucker

Learning Goals:

a. Practice intercultural communication skills.

b. Become aware of various ways meaning is formed in interactions.

Make it Relevant:

Read Chapter 5: "Communicating, Negotiating, and Resolving Conflict Across Cultures."

Get Involved:

Do one of the following activities:

Market Interactions
Go to the market, or to a shop or store or restaurant. Observe how locals interact with vendors: What are greeting forms? Who initiates the interaction? How does the customer ask for something different? Does price negotiation occur? How do interactions conclude?

Speak with a vendor. How long have they been selling the product? How did they become interested in selling the product? How did they gain expertise in the product? What would they like tourists or non-natives to know about the product?

OR

Expressions
Think about a new motto, phrase, or word that you've heard used. Ask or confirm with one or two locals: What does it mean? How

is it used? Is there a popular/historical/cultural basis for its usage? Do they notice when non-native speakers use it or misuse it? Next, think about a communication style or habit in which the locals engage—it may be hand gestures, directness, formalities, interruptions. Ask or confirm with one or two locals: What does it mean? How is it used? Do they notice when non-native speakers use it or misuse it?

Make Sense:

Write a 350- to 500-word essay, summarizing your discoveries from the interaction and reflecting on one or more of the following questions:

Describe differences in gestures, body posture, use of space, use of silence, use of directness, and/or use of politeness, and what those differences communicate.

Describe a time you felt misunderstood. What do you think was the source (or sources) of the miscommunication? Was it language difficulties and word choices, or was it stylistic differences? Have you been able to change your language and/or style to work better in the culture?

Describe a time you offended someone. What did you do wrong? Did the situation escalate because you continued to use US styles and norms, rather than culturally appropriate ones?

A-HA REVELATION: CHANGE YOUR LENS

We each have a *lens*—a set of expectations and judgments, often conditioned by our culture—through which we view the world. Intercultural interactions offer profound opportunities for new understandings and perspectives—for new *lenses*—if we take the time to process the moment.

I call these "a-ha revelations." When you find yourself feeling strong emotions, positive or negative, this is a clue that you have an opportunity to *Change Your LENS*:

Look objectively and List what occurred:

What occurred?

Describe it, and take note of judgmental words (i.e., rude, awful, irritating) or stereotypes.

If there is negativity, eliminate judgmental words, and describe the encounter or event objectively.

Examine your assumptions and Explore inside:

Why did you feel the way you did?

What are the expectations, habits, and beliefs that led you to view the encounter as you did?

Be introspective and describe your attitudes.

Note other possibilities and Nudge yourself to grow:

What other values, habits, and beliefs might be at work here?

Be open-minded and curious. Empathize. Retell the story from another person's perspective. Consider the ways the incident is more complex than you initially realized.

Substantiate with locals and Seek out more:

Is this their truth?

Use your observation, intercultural communication skills, critical thinking skills, and people skills. Ask locals or bicultural people if the new ideas you have generated are accurate, or if there are other parts of the culture you have overlooked.

What else does this make you want to explore? How does this change you and your behaviors, mindsets, and thoughts?

FINAL: MAKE IT MATTER

Read Conclusion: The Essentials of Cultural Intelligence.

Write a thoughtful 350- to 500-word reflection about the following, incorporating your personal experience and the readings.

What do you think it means to be a global citizen? How has your time living abroad given you a better understanding of differing perspectives on civic structures, rights, and responsibilities?

What rights and responsibilities do you have if you are a global citizen? How are you better prepared to be a global citizen because of studying abroad?

APPENDIX B

Making it Creative: Moving Beyond the Classroom

The premise of this manual has been to show how intercultural learning is both academic and experiential. Recognizing that not all educators have the structure of a class to provide learning experiences, this appendix highlights some ways to apply the PRISM to forms and structures outside the class.

You have many, many opportunities to frame students' expectations and learning beyond the class. Once you have determined your learning outcomes, you can think of how to embed them into nearly all of the communication, interactions, and programming you have with students.

Here are just a few ideas.

Get PREPARED: Promotional Materials

What kind of experience do you want your students to have? Help them get prepared for those experiences by framing your promotional materials to reflect this.

Do your photos show your learning outcomes? Do they show students being involved, curious, and respectful? Do your promotional descriptions reflect your learning goals for the students? Do they describe the location like a tourist destination or a learning destination?

The site-seeing aspects and touristy photos and descriptions are undoubtedly part of what makes a location recognizable and appealing to students, and sometimes it is hard to showcase these higher level learning aspects. But you should nonetheless keep an eye on the message the images send, and ways you might be able to showcase your learning goals through photos and descriptions. Your promotional materials set the tone for the experience, and photos and descriptions presenting positive engagement with local people, respect for local sites and traditions, and the exciting ways learning will take place can help students get prepared for intercultural learning.

Make it RELEVANT: Program Information

The program description on your website and brochure is the first resource students have to begin to learn about the intercultural experience. Use this to paint a picture of daily life for the students and connect daily life to the intercultural competency goals of the program. For example:

What are the benefits of the London Program?

As a student, you will be able to develop the following:

- **Increased understanding of international and cultural issues**: Through daily experiences in London shopping, eating, talking, watching TV, and exploring, learn about the British economy, environment, political and social systems, and culture.
- **Increased openness and flexibility**: Living in a small dorm room, using public transportation or walking everywhere, studying in a different academic setting, and other changes will stretch your boundaries in new and rewarding ways.
- **Increased empathy and curiosity**: Speaker's Corner in Hyde Park is not the only place to hear new and challenging ideas. You will be surprised almost daily by new perspectives, values, habits, norms, and attitudes.
- **Enhanced critical skills**: Exploring London, taking courses at a British university, and organizing trips with friends will lead to many new skills: communication, relationships, negotiation, leadership.

Make SENSE: Application Process

Prior to departure, students may not yet be able to articulate their own understanding of the intercultural competence characteristics, because they have not yet had a chance to hone them. But you can set them up for what you hope they will learn.

One way is to encourage them to write a goal or two for their time abroad, and a couple of steps they think will help them. The goal should be something they want to learn or develop or hone. This will prime them to begin thinking of their experience in educational terms.

For further development, send their goals to them while they are abroad.

Get PREPARED: Orientation

Set up the expectation for students to be engaged learners, starting with orientation. Send them *get prepared* quotations ahead of time to reflect on.

Make it RELEVANT: Pre-Departure

Send them resources to Make it Relevant; ask them to come to orientation with at least one question or comment to turn in.

Get INVOLVED: Orientation

Use role-playing and icebreakers at orientations to practice Getting Involved.

Make it MATTER: Code of Conduct

Students should begin to recognize that intercultural competency consists of expectations of behavior. To reinforce this, add these expectations to your Code of Conduct. For example:

TCU international programs strive to incorporate intercultural learning. Life will be different abroad. The following attitudes and behaviors are expected of students participating in the program:

I understand that changes in housing, food, customary practices, transportation, and more will require flexibility and adaptability.

I understand that living in an unfamiliar city, communicating in a different setting or language, and other adaptations will require resourcefulness, problem-solving skills, and people skills.

I understand that being in a foreign country, away from family and familiar resources, will require self-reliance and personal responsibility.

I understand that values and norms may be different, and I will be respectful of others and take advantage of opportunities to learn about those differences.

Get PREPARED: While Abroad

Use social media to post *get prepared* quotations.

Get INVOLVED: While Abroad

Find incentives or requirements for students to participate in local learning activities (i.e., guided museum tours, optional program-organized activities, language partners, etc.). Incentives can include prizes for pix (prizes awarded to students who get pictures of themselves doing these things) or scholarship money for participation.

Make SENSE: Post-Return

Use post-study abroad activities to help students *make sense* and *make their experiences matter.* For example, if you have a photo or video contest, you can find ways to ask how students are making sense of their experiences in their submissions. For example, you can ask that students respond to a learning outcome prompt with their photo submissions.

Use program evaluations to ask students to *make sense* of their experiences. For example:

In what ways do you have a better understanding of your country's

Make Sense: Photo Contest

Category	Learning Outcome Prompts (150-word responses)	Example Photos
Inspirational Insights	How did seeing sites, taking excursions, and exploring the locale help you better understand the country's people, history, religion, politics, or culture?	Monuments, iconic sites, amazing views
Local Life	What was local life like? How did you adapt yourself to be comfortable with the locals?	Students in homestay, students in local cultural activities
Captivated by Culture	What did you find intriguing, unexpected, or even shocking about the people and their culture? What did you learn?	Ceremonies, markets, events
Finding your Footing	What did you do to stretch yourself? What new skills and characteristics did you develop?	Using maps, using new transportation, engaging with locals, taking trips
This Is Study Abroad	What made the experience amazing, transformational, authentic, and *yours*?	You decide

people, economies, environments, political and social systems, values and norms?

How did you adapt your habits to be comfortable in your host city? In what ways did you increase your comfort with people of diverse backgrounds?

In what ways were your values, norms, and behaviors challenged? What did you learn about different ways of being in the world?

What new skills did you develop as a result of this experience?

In what ways are you better prepared to be a global citizen because of studying abroad? How have you been transformed by study abroad?

Make it MATTER

Consider ways to encourage and reward students who continue their learning and involvement.

Promote opportunities for students to engage with local international students or the local international community.

Offer opportunities for them to educate their peers and community through such things as panel discussions, video contests, or educational fairs.

APPENDIX C

Making it Available: Student Handouts

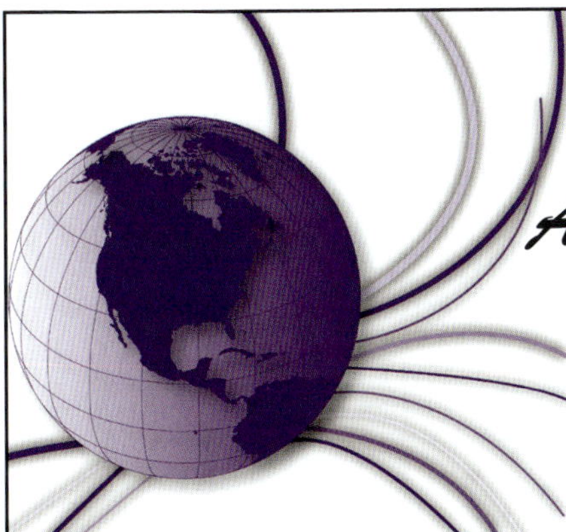

Are you ready to

Look deeper?

See more?

Spark change?

USE the PRISM:

Get PREPARED

Make it RELEVANT

Get INVOLVED

Make SENSE

Make it MATTER

Chart Your Progress

YOUR LEARNING GOALS	GOT PREPARED	MADE IT RELEVANT	GOT INVOLVED	MADE SENSE	MADE IT MATTER

YOUR LEARNING GOALS	GOT PREPARED	MADE IT RELEVANT	GOT INVOLVED	MADE SENSE	MADE IT MATTER

Describe your PRISM

What was your favorite ______?	What did you learn?
What quote or activity has influenced you the most?	
What reading or video has informed you the most?	
What conversation with a local has impacted you the most?	
How has your understanding changed?	
How do you want to apply what you have learned?	

LENS

Change Your LENS

We each have a *lens*—a set of expectations and judgments, often conditioned by our culture—through which we view the world. Intercultural interactions offer profound opportunities for new understandings and perspectives—for new *lenses*—if we take the time to process the moment. I call these "a-ha revelations." When you find yourself feeling strong emotions, positive or negative, this is a clue that you have an opportunity to *Change your LENS:*

Look objectively and List what occurred:

What occurred?

Describe it, and take note of judgmental words (i.e., rude, awful, irritating) or stereotypes.

If there is negativity, eliminate judgmental words, and describe the encounter or event objectively.

Examine your assumptions and Explore inside:

Why did you feel the way you did?

What are the expectations, habits, and beliefs that led you to view the encounter as you did?

Be introspective and describe your attitudes.

Note other possibilities and Nudge yourself to grow:

What other values, habits, and beliefs might be at work here?

Be open-minded and curious. Empathize. Retell the story from another person's perspective. Consider the ways the incident is more complex than you initially realized.

Substantiate with locals and Seek out more:

Is this their truth?

Use your observation, intercultural communication skills, critical thinking skills, and people skills. Ask locals or bicultural people if the new ideas you have generated are accurate, or if there are other parts of the culture you have overlooked.

What else does this make you want to explore? How does this change you and your behaviors, mindsets, and thoughts?

PERMISSIONS

Pyramid Model of Intercultural Competence, p. 5

Reprinted with permission from Sage Publications. From Deardorff, Darla, "Identification and Assessment of Intercultural Competence as a Student Outcome of Internationalization," in *Journal of Studies in International Education*. Copyright 2006 by Darla K. Deardorff.

AAC&U Value Rubric for Intercultural Knowledge and Competency, p. 10

Reprinted with permission from the Association of American Colleges and Universities. From *Assessing Outcomes and Improving Achievement: Tips and Tools for Using Rubrics,* Edited by Terrel L. Rhodes. Copyright 2010 by the Association of American Colleges and Universities.

The Iceberg Concept of Culture, p. 16

Reproduced with permission of AFS Intercultural Programs.

Levels of Influences or Mental Programming, p. 16

Reprinted with permission from Geert Hofstede. From "Culture's Consequences: Comparing Values, Behaviors, Institutions and Organizations Across Nations," Second Edition. Thousand Oaks, California: SAGE Publications, Copyright 2001 by Geert Hofstede.

The Experiential Learning Cycle, p.39

Reprinted with permission from Pearson Education, Inc. From Kolb, David A., *Experiential Learning: Experience as a Source of Learning and Development*, 2nd Ed., New York, New York. Copyright 2015 by David Kolb.

The Form, p. 75

Reproduced with permission of Nicholas Brealey Publishing. From Knight, John and L. Robert Kohls, *Developing Intercultural Awareness*, Copyright 1991, 1994 by John Knight and L. Robert Kohls.

REFERENCES

Introduction

La Brack, Bruce. "What's Up With Culture: On-Line Cultural Training Resource for Study Abroad." *SAFETI (Safety Abroad First - Educational Travel Information) Clearinghouse maintained by the University of Southern California.* 2003. http://www2.pacific.edu/sis/culture/.

Vande Berg, Michael, Jeffrey Connor-Linton, and R. Michael Paige. "The Georgetown Consortium Project: Interventions for Student Learning Abroad." *Frontiers: The Interdisciplinary Journal of Study Abroad* 18, Fall (2009): 1 – 75.

Chapter 1

Adichie, Chimamanda N. "The Danger of a Single Story." *TED Global.* 2009. http://www.ted.com/talks/chimamanda_adichie_the_danger_of_a_single_story

Association of American Colleges and Universities. "AAC&U Intercultural Knowledge and Competence VALUE Rubric." *AAC&U VALUE Rubrics* 2009. https://www.aacu.org/value/rubrics/intercultural-knowledge.

Baron-Cohen, Simon. *The Science of Evil.* New York: Basic Books, 2011.

Bennett, Janet M. "Transformative training: Designing programs for culture learning." In *Contemporary Leadership and Intercultural Competence: Understanding and Utilizing Cultural Diversity to Build Successful Organizations* edited by Michael A. Moodian, 95 – 110. Thousand Oaks, CA: Sage 2008.

Rhodes, Terrel. *Assessing Outcomes and Improving Achievement: Tips and Tools for Using Rubrics.* Washington, DC: Association of American Colleges and Universities 2009.

Deardorff, Darla K. "The Identification and Assessment of Intercultural Competence as a Student Outcome of Internationalization." *Journal of Studies in International Education* 10, no. 3 (2006): 241 – 266.

Deardorff, Darla K. "Intercultural Competence: A Definition, Model, and Implications for Education Abroad." In *Developing Intercultural Competence and Transformation* edited by Victor Savicki, 32 – 52. Sterling, VA: Stylus Publishing 2008.

Deardorff, Darla K. (Ed). *The SAGE Handbook of Intercultural Competence.* Thousand Oaks, CA: Sage Publications, 2009.

Dweck, Carol S. *Mindset: The New Psychology of Success.* New York: Random House, 2006.

Flanagan, Linda. "How Improv Can Open up the Mind to Learning in the Classroom and Beyond." *Mind/Shift.* January 30 2015. https://ww2.kqed.org/mindshift/2015/01/30/how-improv-can-open-up-the-mind-to-learning-in-the-classroom-and-beyond/

Grunzweig, Walter and Nana Rinehart. "International Understanding and Global Interdependence: A philosophical inquiry." *International Educator,* Fall (1998): 41-48.

Guadagnoli, Mark, Marie-Paul Morin, and Adam Dubrowski. "The Application of the Challenge Point Framework in Medical Education." *Medical Education,* 46 (2012): 447-453.

Gudykunst, William B. *Bridging Differences.* Thousand Oaks, CA: Sage Publications, 2009.

Gudykunst, William, Stella Ting-Toomey and Richard Wiseman. "Taming the Beast: Designing a Course in Intercultural Communication." *Communication Education,* 40 (1991): 272-285.

Haidt, Jonathan. *The Happiness Hypothesis.* New York: Basic Books, 2006.

Hall, Edward. T. *Beyond Culture.* Garden City, NY: Anchor Press / Doubleday, 1976.

Hoefstede, Geert. *Culture's Consequences: International Differences in Work-Related Values.* Beverly Hills, CA: Sage Publications, 1980.

Hunter, Amy. "Transformative Learning in International Education." In *Developing Intercultural Competence and Transformation* edited by Victor Savicki, 92 – 107. Stylus: Sterling, VA 2008.

Kashdan, Todd. *Curious? Discover the Missing Ingredient to a Fulfilling Life.* New York: HarperCollins, 2009.

Kim, Yong Yun "Intercultural Communication Competence: A Systems-Theoretic View." In *Cross-cultural Interpersonal Communication* edited by Stella Ting-Toomey and Felipe Korzenny, 259 – 275. Newbury Park: Sage Publications 1991.

Kohls, L. Robert. *The Values Americans Live by*. Washington, DC: Meridian House International, 1984.

Peace Corps. *Building Bridges: A Peace Corps Classroom Guide to Cross-Cultural Understanding*. Washington DC: Paul D. Coverdell World Wise Schools, 2002.

Pedersen, Paul B. and Mark Pope. "Inclusive Cultural Empathy for Successful Global Leadership." *American Psychologist*, November, (2010): 841-854.

Rifkin, Jeremy. "RSA Animate: The Empathic Civilisation." *The RSA*. May 6, 2010. https://www.youtube.com/watch?v=l7AWnfFRc7g&feature=youtu.be.

Rubin, Donald L. and Richard Sutton. "Assessing Student Learning Outcomes from Study Abroad." *International Educator* 10, no. 2 (2001): 30-31.

Spolin, Viola. *Theatre Games for the Classroom: A Teacher's Handbook*. Evanston: Northwestern UP, 1986.

Sanford, Nevitt. *The American College*. New York: Wiley, 1962.

Stori, Craig. *Cross-Cultural Dialogues: 74 Brief Encounters with Cultural Difference*. Boston, MA: Nicholas Brealey Publishing, 1994.

Suthakaran, Veerasamy. "Using Analogies to Enhance Self-Awareness and Cultural Empathy: Implications for Supervision." *Journal of Multicultural Counseling and Development* 39, no. 4 (2011): 206-217.

Vande Berg, Michael, R. Michael Paige and Kris Hemming Lou (eds.) *Student Learning Abroad: What Our Students Are Learning, What They're Not, and What We Can Do About It*. Sterling, VA: Stylus 2012.

Wesch, Michael. "From Knowledgeable to Knowledge-Able: Learning in New Media Environments." *Academic CommonsAcademic Commons*. 2009. http://www.academiccommons.org/from-knowledgable-to-knowledge-able-learning-in-new-media-environments/

Zhu, Honglin. "From Intercultural Awareness to Intercultural Empathy." *English Language Teaching, 4* (1) 2011: 116-119.

Chapter 2

Adichie, Chimamanda N. "The Danger of a Single Story." *TED Global*. 2009. http://www.ted.com/talks/chimamanda_adichie_the_danger_of_a_single_story

Anderson, Lorin W. and David R. Krathwohl. *A Taxonomy for Learning, Teaching, and Assessing: A Revision of Bloom's Taxonomy of Educational Objectives*. Addison Wesley Longman, Inc., 2001.

Bruner, Jerome. "Frames for Thinking. Ways of Making Meaning." In *Modes of Thought; Explorations in Culture and Cognition* edited by David R. Olson and Nancy Torrance, 93-105. Cambridge, UK: Cambridge University Press 1996.

Carey, Benedict. *How We Learn: The Surprising Truth about When, Where and Why It Happens.* New York: Random House, 2014.

Fenwick, Tara. "Inside Out of Experiential Learning: Fluid Bodies, Co-emergent Minds." In *Learning Outside the Academy: International Research Perspectives on Lifelong Learning* edited by Richard Edwards, Jim Gallagher and Susan Whittaker, 42 – 55. New York: Routledge 2006.

Fink, L. Dee "Transforming Students Through High Impact Teaching Practices." Presented at *AAEEBL Western Regional Conference*, Texas Christian University. February 29, 2016.

Fink, L. Dee. *Creating Significant Learning Experiences, Revised and Updated.* San Francisco, CA: Jossey-Bass, 2013.

Fogg, Brian J. "Persuasive Technologies." *Communication of the ACM* 42, no. 5 (1999): 27-29.

Guthrie, Kathy L. and Tamara Betrand Jones. "Teaching and Learning: Using Experiential Learning Reflection for Leadership Education." *New Directions for Student Services,* Winter 140 (2012): 53-63.

Hatcher, Julie A. and Robert G. Bringle. "Reflection: Bridging the Gap between Service and Learning." *College Teaching* 45, no. 4 Fall (1997): 153-158.

Hattie, John and Yates, Gregory. *Visible Learning and the Science of How We Learn*. New York: Routledge, 2013.

Hatton, Neville and David Smith. "Reflection in Teacher Education: Towards Definition and Implementation." *Teaching and Teacher Education* 11, no. 1 (1995): 33-49.

Hoey, Brian. "A Simple Introduction to the Practice of Ethnography and Guide to Ethnographic Fieldnotes." *Marshall University Digital Scholar,* 2014. http://works.bepress.com/brian_hoey/12/

Jordi, Richard. "Reframing the Concept of Reflection: Consciousness, Experiential Learning, and Reflective Learning Practices." *Adult Education Quarterly* 61, no. 2 (2011): 181-197.

Kennison, Monica. "Developing Reflective Writing as Effective Pedagogy." *Nursing Education Perspectives* 3, no. 5 (2012): 306-311.

Kennison, Monica and Shirley Misselwitz. "Evaluating Reflective Writing for Appropriateness, Fairness, and Consistency." *Nursing Education Perspectives* 23, no. 5 (2002): 238-242.

Kolb, David A. *Experiential Learning: Experience as the Source of Learning and Development, Second Edition.* Upper Saddle River, New Jersey: Pearson Education, 2015.

Kolb, David. A. *Experiential Learning: Experience as the Source of Learning and Development.* Upper Saddle River, New Jersey: Prentice Hall, 1984.

Mair, Carolyn. "Using Technology for Enhancing Reflective Writing, Metacognition and Learning." *Journal of Further and Higher Education* 32, no. 2 (2012): 147-167.

Mintz, Joseph and Morten Aagaard. "The Application of Persuasive Technology to Educational Settings." *Education Tech Research Development* 60, (2012): 483-499.

Moon, Jennifer A. *A Handbook of Reflective and Experiential Learning.* New York: Routledge Falmer, 2004.

Moore, Donna T. "Forms and Issues in Experiential Learning." *New Directions for Teaching and Learning* Winter, 124 (2010): 3-13.

Novak, Gregor. M. "Just-in-Time Teaching." *New Directions for Teaching and Learning* 128, (2011): 63-73.

Stand Up Kids. 2015. http://standupkids.org/standing-vs-sitting/. Retrieved 05/26/2016.

Smith, Elizabeth. "Teaching Critical Reflection." *Teaching in Higher Education* 16, no. 2 (2011): 211-223.

Wagner, Kenneth and Tony Magistrale. *Writing Across Culture: An Introduction to Study Abroad and the Writing Process.* New York: Peter Lang, 2000.

ABOUT THE AUTHOR

Photo by Todd Rundstrom

TRACY RUNDSTROM WILLIAMS is the associate director of the Center for International Studies at TCU, where she teaches courses on global citizenship and oversees the Global Academy. Her study abroad and teaching abroad experience spans the globe, and her research on intercultural learning, including the "Change Your LENS" process for understanding intercultural encounters, has been widely adapted.